WEIGHTING FOR WINNERS

BY JIM ADAMS

ISBN 978-0-9552171-5-9

Published by Sportsworld Publishing,
Raines House, Denby Dale Road,
Wakefield, WF1 1HL

www.sportsworldpublishing.co.uk

Cover by Gable Lake Design

Typeset by Kaye Hooson, Network
Management Solutions ltd.

Official scale of Weight for Age

	5 fur	6 fur
Mar 16-31	12	13
Apr 1-15	11	12
Apr 16-30	10	11
May 1-15	9	10
May 16-31	8	9
June 1-15	7	8
June 16-30	6	7
July 1-15	5	6
July 16-31	4	5
Aug 1-15	3	4
Aug 16-31	2	3
Sept 1-15	1	2
Sept 16-30	1	2
Oct 1-15	0	1
Oct 16-31	0	1
Nov 1-15	0	0

This scale demonstrates that the weight-for-age allowance that a 3yo would receive from an older horse over 5 furlongs on June 10th is 7lbs, whereas over the same distance on September 17th the allowance is only 1 lb. Similarly, a 3yo against an older horse on April 18th over 6 furlongs will receive 11 lbs but on July 2nd only 6 lbs. From November 1st onwards the allowance is nil.

Author's Note:

My grateful thanks are due to Raceform Ltd for their kind permission to use their race numbers and to quote the comments of their race readers.

Weighting for Winners

CHAPTER ONE

The handicapping of racehorses by the allocation of differing weights in accordance with their racing ability is not an exact science and this is due to the circumstance that the decisions taken to allot a rating, a task done by the Official Handicapper (OH), are almost entirely a matter of opinion, albeit one which is backed up by years of expertise and experience.

It is in the nature of things that some racehorses are better, i.e. faster, than their equine companions and, unless there was some way of giving even the slowest some chance of winning, horse racing as we know it would cease to exist as the fastest would win all the time.

Over a very long time it has been found that the most satisfactory way of equalising the chances for each horse is to set the inherently faster horses to carry more weight than their less talented colleagues. But how much more weight? As Shakespeare would say, that is the question.

After years of experience and many thousands of actual races it has been generally accepted that over say, five or six furlongs, an allowance of 3lbs per length is the norm. Thus, if horse A beat horse B a length at level weights, they could theoretically be brought together by the slightly better horse being asked to concede 3lbs in weight the next time they met.

This accepted weight allowance of 3lbs per length does not however apply to all distances and on all kinds of ground conditions. Over 2 miles and in soft going a more likely allowance would be around 1lb per length, which means of course that, over different distances and going, there would be a notional scale of allowances to be applied as a rough guide.

Again, all of this is a matter of opinion and it is thus perfectly acceptable for any impartial observer to disagree with that of the O.H. It can be said that the result of every handicap "proves" the handicapper wrong in that the result is never the multiple dead-heat aimed for, except that to point to this fact as proof that the official was "wrong" would be a harsh judgment. Racehorses improve but they can also deteriorate and the result of any race can be affected by these and factors such as luck in running, the going and perhaps the draw. A racehorse will often run to the official rating but it can equally run above or below its figure.

After each handicap the OH has to re-assess the ratings and make such amendments as are indicated by the result of the race. To do this, the OH generally makes a judgment as to which of the first horses to finish have run to form and so provide a benchmark upon which to revise the ratings. A fresh rating cannot be pulled out of the air and a horse rated at say 80, is hardly likely to be re-assessed on the 100 mark and his or her new figure would usually be consistent with a previous rating. Thus, in order to allot new ratings, it is necessary to take a retrospective view of the horse's past performances. If a horse has earned consecutive ratings of say 80, 82, 81.79 and 78, its new rating would be in line with his latest figures unless he or she put up a performance bordering on the miraculous.

In my own handicap workings I have found many sprinters who run to within a pound or two of their mark time after time and these admirably consistent animals are worth their weight in gold to any handicapper, professional or otherwise, as they can be used as a reliable guide to the form of the race.

In order to make any attempt to compile one's own handicap, one therefore needs a reliable data base of ratings in order to make any sort of judgment.

Here, one must draw attention to the different approach between that of the amateur handicapper and that of the professional. The Jockey Club handicapper is constrained by circumstances which necessarily temper his thinking. If any horse finishes four lengths behind the winner in a sprint handicapper and connections entertain the notion that he will be downgraded some 12 lbs on the strength of the notional 3lbs per length, one can only say, dream on! It is very rare for a horse to be downgraded by more than a couple of pounds on the strength of one below par performance and the general practice is for a horse to go down in the ratings by very small adjustments and over a considerable length of time.

Handicappers are very shrewd and knowledgeable men and know that to downgrade a horse by more than a couple of pounds as the result of one performance would open the floodgates to a few wide awake trainers who would see this as a way of getting their charge on a much lower handicap mark.

There is perhaps no justice in the treatment accorded to an easy winner and a sparkling performance in a good race will undoubtedly get clobbered by the OH who will cheerfully put its rating up 10 lbs or more. A backroom lawyer could plead that this is unfair discrimination against winners, as a 6 length winner's rating is affected much more than the figure allotted to a six lengths loser but this is the way it has to be. It would be a dereliction of duty by the OH if he were to make it easy for an improving horse to set up a long winning run in one handicap race after another.

The amateur handicapper is not bound by these same hindrances however and, in the privacy of his own home and in his little books he can do what he likes and if a horse runs what he considers to be 10lbs below its best, he can show this without fear or favour. His decisions do not affect the official ratings and the amateur has the luxury of letting his figures show what has actually happened. For this reason, a succession of ratings shown against one horse by the amateur is a truer reflection of the actual performances than those of the OH whose work is not only subject to scrutiny by professionals but has to stand up against future performances of the animal in question.

In practice however, it is not necessary to re-asses a horse by deducting as much as 10lb from its rating and one with an official rating of say, 80, can safely be give a pro-tem figures of 73?, which clearly indicates that it has run well below form and that an exact rating cannot safely be allotted.

It need hardly be said that calculating the actual ratings for the top horses to finish calls for knowledge, experience and a modicum of luck. Setting one's opinion against a highly skilled Official Handicapper calls for confidence in one's own judgment but it is well worth making the effort. One has to bear in mind that, as outlined above, the OH has not got an entirely free hand and either in watching the race or reading the form book, he has only the same facts upon which to make a judgment. It is perfectly true that the official sees far more racing than the average person and doubtless also has access to videos of races which he has not been able to see, but a skilled interpreter of the form book assisted by the invaluable comments of the professional race-readers, has enough information at his or her disposal to compete on almost level terms.

Earlier in this book reference was made to having a reliable data base of information upon which to formulate one's opinion, and it is obvious that one needs an up to date record of race results which contain all that is necessary, including extended distances.   There is no better way of finding this information than in the Official Form Book published by Raceform, or of course, the Results Section of the Raceform Update published by the same company. These invaluable publications contain not only all the data required but contain quite invaluable comments by highly skilled race readers. In forming an opinion of the result of a race one needs to know not only what won and by how much but also HOW it won,

When a horse wins by ½ length one needs to know not just that mathematical fact, but also whether the win was gained by a horse absolutely flat out or in its own comfort zone and won, as the expression goes, hard held.   If one is to make any sort of weight allowance for a winning distance it is vital to know in what manner the win was achieved and the professional comments in Raceform are without equal in this respect.

After every race in which one is interested, the Results Section of either of these publications can be used as a repository for one's own ratings simply by inserting it by the side of the horse's name. It will be necessary to keep a record of one's findings as one needs to be able to have ready access to a list containing the names of the horses but also the successive ratings they have earned during the season.

For this purpose the author has successfully used a computer based spreadsheet upon which entries can be made on a day-to-day basis. A typical entry would read:

Blue Dragon   80/84/83/78/80

with each backslash showing the side by side columns of the spreadsheet.

If every horse were to earn a rating every time it ran there would be no problem but unfortunately this is not the case as they are not always in the first six. There is also the problem that many of "our" horses run in races other than Class 1, 2 or 3 handicaps and, in order not to be caught out by this circumstance it is necessary also to show this in one's records on the spreadsheet.

So, a fairly typical entry might now read:

Forked Lightning   90/88/Cl4 0/Lis/92/Cl4 2/AW

At first glance this is an example of gobbledegook but is easily explained, although it has to be said that the various signs and symbols are the author's own invention.

The first two numbers are obviously the ratings earned by Forked Lightning. "Cl4 0" simply indicates that it ran in a Class 4 handicap and finished unplaced. The symbol "Lis" means that he next ran in a listed race, whilst we then get a normal rating of 92. He then ran in another Class 4 handicap but finished second and the final entry "AW" shows he ran at an all-weather track, the result of which does not interest us.

A detailed record like this, which is easily kept up to date on a day-to-day basis, shows at a glance what the animal has been doing apart from running in one of our selected races. There is a good reason why this additional data is required. There are many times when a horse earns a rating of say, 98 early in the season and then, for various reasons, runs in races other than our chosen events, in Listed races, or on the all-weather tracks and, unless one has a quick, visual guide to this behaviour, one can easily use an very old rating, perhaps one which the horse can no longer run up to. It also helps with the old age problem of how far back to go in deciding to use a rating as a guide to a current race. If your record shows that the first rating of say 98 has been swallowed up by subsequent events, the figure you have could easily be out of date. One way to avoid being caught by surprise in this way is to keep an eye on such an entry and if there are more than two or three items since the last bona fide figure, then have a quick look at the Ratings List published in both the Form Book and the Raceform Update, and see if the horse in question is entered for a race that week. If so, check the Official Rating and compare with the latest entry on your sheet. Any large discrepancy and you will have been warned and know that things are not what they seem.

It might be wondered why a private handicapper is advised to deal only with the first six horses but this is easily explained. Under the Rules of Racing, jockeys are compelled to ride their mounts out to secure the best possible placing but no Steward would want to see a horse being thrashed when it obviously has no chance of even getting a place. In sprint handicaps the finishes are invariably quite close and a furlong out there would be quite a few horses with a reasonable chance and one can safely assume that the first six horses have been ridden out as demanded by the rules.

If one studies the work of the OH, it is quite clear that the ratings of horses finishing out of the first six are seldom amended by more than a couple of pounds or so and those finishing a long way behind are never given more than a token allowance. The biggest alterations are always made to the ratings of the first three or four horses to finish and extending this to the first six is a quite reasonable practice for the private handicapper. The one besetting problem is to know how to allot one's own ratings to those horses which qualify for attention and perhaps the best way to do this is to examine a few actual races.

Readers will see that all the races dealt with are sprint handicaps and only those from Class 3 up are covered. Not all these handicaps are dealt with analytically but only those which serve to illustrate a particular point, or highlight an individual horse are included. Due to this, the races are not in numerical order as the book is not intended to show every handicap race within our terms of reference.

For this reason, it is not possible to run backwards for a horse's complete yearly record but this was never the intention. It is self evident that WFA events are not included, although this means that some of the top sprint races of the year are not included. Over a period of many years, the author and others have found that the form shown in handicaps is not compatible with that shown in WFA events although there is no clear reason why this is so. It is a known fact that horses will show form in WFA races which simply does not translate to handicaps. We are endeavouring to compile a running handicap of those horses which run against each other on handicap terms and to introduce any race where they meet on level terms would just complicate matters as they could well produce some very odd results.

CHAPTER THREE

It is now proposed to do an analysis of many sprint handicaps run during the 2008 season and it should be made clear that these are not necessarily in any chronological order but have been selected to illustrate interesting points of handicapping.

The first example we look at is a race which resulted in a win for the joint-top rated horse and meant taking a look at the past records of those taking part.

The race under survey is the Goodwood Revival Meeting Stakes Handicap run at Goodwood on August 23, where the first six horses were as follows:

Race 5270

Class 3		6 furs.	Good to soft		Post race ratings
	Osiris Way	6.9.4	87		90
½	Mujood	5.9.7	90		91
Hd	Seamus Shindig	6.9.3	86		86
¾	Rash Judgement	3.8.12	84		82
¾	Thebes	3.9.5	91		87
3	Berbice	3.9.4	90		83?

A brief note about Weight-for Age (WFA)

The official allowance for a 3yo against older horses in the second half of August is 3lbs.

In the above race Rash Judgement is set to carry 5lbs less than Seamus Shindig (rated 86) so this puts it on a figure of $81 + 3 = 84$. There is no real need to concern yourself with this as the WFA allowance is automatically taken into account when the weights are allotted.

Note: Apprentice allowances are ignored.

Our past ratings were:	Osiris Way	85/85/87/89
	Mujood	No figure
	Seamus Shindig	No figure
	Rash Judgement	86/83/82/86
	Thebes	92
	Berbie	No figure
	Merlin's Dancer	85
	Film Maker	87
	Idle Power	81/83

Comparison against the official ratings showed the following top rated horses:

Osiris Way	-2	Won 5-1
Rash Judgement	-2	
Merlin's Dancer	-1	
Idle Power	-	

In studying the result and comments on the race, it seemed likely that Seamus Shindig who stayed on well in the last stages, had run to his rating of 91 and, if we take this as a marker, we get the following new ratings:

Rash Judgement down 2lbs
Seamus Shindig stays on 86
Mujood up 1lb
Osiris Way up 3lbs to 90
Berbice goes down a doubtful 7lbs to 83?

The new ratings are very close to the revised official figures but one would expect this to be the case, whilst Berbice, beaten three lengths by the fifth Thebes only goes down by 3lbs. Thus, the result of the race and the revised placings are entirely within expectations and we can be satisfied that they will act as a good guide for the future.

We next take the EBF Chichester Observer Fillies' Stakes (Handicap), also run at Goodwood

Race 5310

Class 3	6 furs.	Soft going	Post race ratings	
	Perfect Flight	3.8.5	77	83
3	Superduper	3.8.10	82	82
Sh hd	Maimoona	3.9.3	89	89
3 ¾	Janina	3.9.6	92	85?
2	Angus Newz	5.9.9	92	85?
6	Temple of Thebes	3.9.2	88	81?

The past ratings were:	Perfect Flight	78
	Superduper	No figure
	Maimoona	86
	Janina	No figure
	Angus Newz	89/83
	Temple of Thebes	88

Set against the official ratings we get:	Perfect Flight	-1	Won 10-1
	Temple of Thebes	-	
	Maimoona	+3	
	Angus Newz	+3	

Not a good race and, in soft going, one could hardly be confident, but Perfect Flight was well suited by the conditions and drew away at the finish to win by a comfortable 3 lengths. The extended distances, with nearly 15 lengths between the first and sixth horses, did not bode well for any amendments and the following are as much guesswork as anything else.

Maimoona had won easily in soft going at Ripon on her previous outing and we were inclined to take the view that she and Superduper had probably run to their official ratings and the following amendments were made;

Perfect Flight goes up 6lbs for 3 lengths to 83, Superduper and Maimoona stay on their official ratings of 82 and 89, whilst the rest all go down a notional 7lbs with a query for doubt. In view of her pre-race rating, Temple of Thebes must be adjudged as having run well below her best and there may have been a reason for her poor showing.

The next race in which we take an interest is a prestigious sprint run at Ripon, the result of which confirms the general feeling that you can never overlook anything trained by Dandy Nicholls.

Great St Wilfred Stakes   (Heritage Handicap)

Race 5109

Class 2   Ripon   6furs.   Good to soft   Post race ratings

The result was as follows:

	Tajneed	5.8.12	92	96
	Tajneed	5.8.12	92	96
Hd	Valery Borzov	4.9.4	98	100
Nk	Tamagin	5.9.3	97	99
¾	Conquest	4.9.6	100	101
3 ¼	Confuchias	4.9.6	100	96?
1	Patavellian	10.9.3	97	92?

At this point it has to be pointed out that, in order to cut down on the work load, the author had earlier taken the decision to concentrate on Class 1, 2 and 3 sprint handicaps only and to ignore those scheduled under Class 4,5 and 6. Apart from the time involved, it was felt that the vast majority of horses running in the latter races are of such poor quality that they were simply not worth the additional work. Unfortunately, this can mean that a horse putting up a good performance in say, a Class 4 race does not earn a rating.

In the case of the winner, he had run in a Class 3 handicap at Doncaster earlier in the year and this was the result:

Race 1300

Class 3		6 furs.	Good to soft		Post race ratings
	Cape	5.8.11	88		92
Nk	Baby Strange	4.8.8	85		88
Nk	Tajneed	5.8.4	81		83
½	Damika	5.9.4	95		96
NK	Bel Cantor	5.8.4	81		81
Hd	Turnkey	6.9.0	91		91
2	Pusey Street Lady	4.9.2	93		89

The post-race figures were subsequently proved to be reasonably correct for most of these horses and the figure of 83 for Tajneed could hardly be faulted. Unfortunately for our peace of mind, Tajneed's next race was in the Class 4 Levy Board handicap run over 6 furs at Ripon. He simply stormed home by 4 ½ lengths but of course, this race was not rated with us. As a result of this race Tajneed went up to an official rating of 94 and on that rating he ran in a Class 2 race at Newmarket but failed to live up to his figure and finished 11th.

When we came to the Great St Wilfred therefore, Nicholls' gelding was a lowly 83 with us although he was clearly better than that and was also a course and distance winner. In view of his splendid win at this course on a previous occasion, his win, ridden by the trainer's son Adrian, was hardly a tremendous shock even though he was "not rated" with us. The moral of this series of events is that one has to sit up and take notice of any horse which wins a lower class race by a mind boggling 4 ½ lengths. Fortunately this sort of thing doesn't happen very often and we continue to leave Class 4,5 and 6 un-rated with the proviso that, in assessing the chances of the runners in a higher class race, it is always wise to run a rough check on any un-rated horse which has been showing good form. It is easy to be wise after the event. Incidentally, the disappointment of the Great St Wilfred was Baby Strange, of which more later.

Now we come to a race which raises the perennial question of how far back does one go in calculating the ratings for any particular race? The race in question is the Bluesquarecom Stewards' Cup at Goodwood, one of the most prestigious sprint handicaps in the calendar.

Race 4624

Class 3	6 furs.	Good	Post race assessments

This was the result:

	Conquest	4.8.9	95	101
Hd	King's Apostle	4.9.2	102	107
½	Borderlescott	6.9.10	110	114
2 ½	Machinist	8.8.11	97	97
½	Mac Gill Eoin	4.9.0	100	98
Nk	Knot in Wood	6.8.12	98	98

When the time came to make our pre-race assessments, the only rating available for Conquest was an early 96 when he finished fifth on an official rating of 99 to Viking Spirit over 6 furs at Goodwood in May. If one took any notice of this early rating, Conquest was actually top rated with us at -1. At 40-1 this was something to drool over but wiser (?) counsel prevailed.

Since that run at Goodwood in May, Conquest had run three times. On a rating of 99 he had finished 13th in the Royal Ascot Wokingham Stakes and then, on his next run and, according to the Raceform race-reader, he gave an "unenthusiastic" display when 7th in a Class 2 handicap at Windsor. On his final out before taking part in the Stewards' Cup, Conquest stumbled at the start over 6 fur at Chepstow and finished 11th of 12, having been in the rear all the way.

With the best will in the world, it was hard to fancy our top rated horse and there were mixed feelings when he beat the unlucky King's Apostle by a neck. Since that win, Conquest has shown that he has taken on a new lease of life by finishing a very good fourth in the Great St Wilfred (mentioned earlier) on a new rating of 100. It is quite clear that our early rating of 96 was spot on at the time as he subsequently proved himself at least 5 lbs better than that.

Our general rule would be to ignore a rating that is more than a couple of months old unless there is clear evidence that the horse has not deteriorated and is still capable of producing an early rating. Unfortunately, in Conquest's race there was little of encouragement in three subsequent races to suggest that he was up to winning the Steward's Cup and so went un-backed. There is really no lesson to be learned as common sense dictates that a decent recent showing is most desirable in dealing with any horse race and that months old form is not to be relied upon. However, I will deal with this aspect of private handicapping later on in this book.

If there is any moral to be found in any of this, it is that course and distance winners are always worth a second look

NOTES

_____
_____
_____
_____
_____
_____
_____
_____
_____
_____
_____
_____
_____
_____
_____
_____
_____
_____
_____
_____
_____
_____
_____
_____
_____

CHAPTER FOUR

Readers may by now, have wondered if races at all-weather tracks are worthy of our attention and it has to be said that, unlike the early days of these tracks, the class of animals running is often very good. However, it is indicative of the difference between these composite surfaces and good English turf that the official handicappers often give two separate ratings for horses which go from one to another. Some horses adapt to both surfaces but many of them prefer one or the other and because one can never be sure whether the form at one type of track will transfer to another, the author never entertains all-weather form in summing up for a turf event. There is nothing personal in this but no serious backer of horses needs to introduce a further cause for uncertainty.

Past readers of my books on handicapping have asked why the specialisation in 5 and 6 furlong handicaps and the question deserves an answer. Concentrating on one section of the horse population enables one to become very familiar with the form of not too many horses and even those with their various quirks become old friends. Quite apart from this, sprint handicaps are contested by horses who know only one way to run and from a long experience of handicapping these races, it can be said that most of those taking part are astonishingly consistent. Quite a large number of sprinters run their races out to within a pound or two of their rating time after time. These paragons of virtue are like gold dust to any handicapper, private or professional, and in many races the new ratings can be calculated by using one of them as a benchmark to confirm the general pattern of the figures so that they "look right".

As readers will also know, the apprentice allowance is disregarded in calculating ratings and this is the practice adopted by the Official Handicappers. A horse set to carry 9.5, who actually carries 8.12 when ridden by a 7lb claimer, is always assessed on its original weight. The difference in weight is said to compensate for the lack of experience, but from long observation, the author can say that many a top rated horse has been transformed into a "steering job" by the employment of a good apprentice. Students of handicapping are advised never to be put off if a horse well in at the weights on one's figures is ridden by an apprentice with a claim. The golden rule really is that if the rider is good enough for the trainer, he or she is good enough for the punter.

One great advantage of compiling one's own handicap is that the successive ratings clearly indicate an improving horse. Such an animal is that useful sprinter Baby Strange, whose form figures on my spreadsheet go - 88/85/85/90/90/88/97/99. It was therefore quite surprising when the grey colt failed to make any impression in the Great St Wilfred at Ripon on an official rating of 97 (-2 with us), and finished down the field in 10th place. One observer took the view that he was a little high in the weights but the colt's form in the Scottish Stewards' Cup and the Goodwood Stewards' Sprint Stakes showed the horse to be well up to winning the Great St Wilfred and he was well backed at 6-1 to do so. It might be he had had enough for the time being. A similar case was that of the Tim Easterby trained gelding, Hamish McGonagall, whose first outing this year was in the Thomas Lord Handicap at Thirsk in April. The result is shown here.

Race 1484

Class 3   5 furs.   Good (Good to soft in places)   Post race ratings

	Mey Blossom	3.9.4	85	89
½	Hamish McGonagall	3.9.0	81	84
1 ¼	Rose Slog	3.8.12	79	79
¾	Cape Vale	3.9.2	83	81
Nk	President Elect	3.8.9	76	74
1 ¾	Style Award	3.9.4	85	80

The resolution of these placings was done through the third horse, Rose Slog, who showed up well throughout and kept on well under pressure. There seemed no good reason to change the filly's rating of 79, which, allowing 3lbs for the 1 ¼ lengths separating them, put Hamish

McGonagall on the 84 mark. This in turn put the winner on 89 and with the fourth horse being only ¾ lengths behind the third a drop of 2 lbs is about right, with the same amount being taken off President Elect. Style Award did not have a clear run so we take just 5lbs off his rating. Hamish McGonagall had seemingly trained on and confirmed this with his next out when he won the Axis Intermodal Handicap at York.

Race 2171

Class 3	5 furs.	Good to firm	Post race ratings	
	Hamish McGonagall	3.9.3	84	87
Hd	Lesson in Humility	3.9.6	87	89
¾	Marvellous Value	3.9.4	85	85
1	Style Award	3.9.3	84	82
½	Rash Judgement	3.9.5	86	83
1 ¼	Grudge	3.8.4	71	66

Raceform's race-reader thought that Marvellous Value had run to his best, so leaving him on the official mark of 85 seemed justified. Lesson in Humility also ran a fine race and was in front a few yards past the line, so a rise of 2lbs for the ¾ length was his reward, which puts Hamish McGonagall, a very narrow winner just 3lbs up on the 87 mark. Style Award goes down to 82 and Grudge, whose rider put up 3 o.w. drops down to 66. Hamish McGonagall who had won over 5 fur at York, appeared not to stay the 6th furlong in the Betfair Sprint at the same course, but bounced back with an excellent second in the 5 fur Gosforth Cup at Newcastle.

Race 3451

			Good to soft		Post race ratings
	Buachaill Dona	5.9.12	98		102
1	Hamish McGonaghall	3.8.12	90		91
Hd	Pusey Street Lady	4.9.4	90		90
1 ½	How's She Cuttin'	5.8.11	83		80
½	Fathom Five	4.9.11	97		93
Nk	Dig Deep	6.8.12	84		79

Class 2   5 furs.

At the line Pusey Street Lady was pushing Hamish McGonagall for second place and is deemed to have to right up to her official rating of 90 which put the second on the 91 mark, representing an improvement of some 7lbs on his last outing. The fourth, fifth and sixth all go down in accordance with their beaten distances. Hamish McGonagall then improved even further when, well drawn, he won the Kathleen B Corbett Handicap over 5 furs at Chester.

Race 3909

Class 3   5 furs.   Good to soft   Post race ratings

	Hamish McGonaghall	3.9.3	91	98
1	Requisite	3.8.6	80	85
2 ½	Little Pete	3.9.0	88	88
1 ½	Thunder Bay	3.8.9	83	80
½	Fol Hollow	3.9.7	95	91
1 ½	Cake	3.9.7	95	89

Getting a handle on the form of this race was made easier by the presence of Little Pete, who has been running to the 88 mark since the start of the season. On good to soft going the 2½ lengths beating that Requisite gave Little Pete was worth a minimum of 5 lbs, thus putting the second on the 85 mark with an extra 2 lbs, making a total of 7 lbs added to the winner's rating of 91. Using Little Pete as the benchmark put Thunder Bay on about 80, with Fol Hollow going down to 91 and Cake on 89.

The OH was less slightly impressed with the winner's performance and, in the Ratings List after this race, he was put on the 96 mark. He was thus treated even more favourably in the Giles Insurance Stakes, a Class 2 Heritage handicap run over 5 furlongs at Ayr and Hamish McGonagall was second favourite at 13-2 to score. According to Raceform, he looked in very good shape and was right up there till just over a furlong out, then weakened quite quickly to finish 14th of the 16 runners. He had shown improvement and this was a disappointing showing for which there was no obvious excuse. Unfortunately, these things happen in the best regulated circles. However Justice was done in the last race in this book.

Mention of Little Pete in the foregoing analysis brings to mind the Turf Club handicap over 5 furlongs at Goodwood, in which he finished second to Piscean when conceding that horse no less than 13 lbs.

Race 4591

Class 3	5 furs.	Good to firm		Post race ratings
	Picean	3.8.3	75	81
nse	Little Pete	3.9.2	88	94
2 ¼	Cake	3.9.6	92	92
Nk	Rash Judgement	3.9.1	87	86
¾	Fol Hollow	3.9.7	93	92
1	Good Gorsoon	3.9.5	91	89

We had good, reliable figures for most of these and we took Cake as being the one to go by. She showed speed to be up with the leaders for most of the way and stayed on well under pressure.

She finished 2 ¼ lengths behind Little Pete which put him on the 94 mark some 6 lbs over his usual niche of 88. Nevertheless, the form looked solid enough and the rest were adjusted through Cake. The OH however, put Little Pete on the 92 mark and he was on that level when he next ran in the good class Shergar Cup Sprint handicap over 6 furlongs at Ascot.

Race 4842

				Post race ratings
Class 2	6 furs.	Soft Going		
	Shifting Star	3.9.6	92	96
1 ¼	Al Muheer	3.9.12	98	98
1	Kaldoun Kingdom	3.9.5	91	90
Nk	Spanish Bounty	3.9.10	96	95
2	Spitfire	3.9.12	98	94
¾	Little Pete	3.9.6	92	88+

Al Muheer, who is probably better at further, ran a solid race to be up there all the way and looked likely to have run right up to his official rating of 98. He was a length and a quarter behind the winner who was, however, receiving 6lb and balancing one against the other puts the winner on a rating of about 96. Kaldoun Kingdom goes down 1lb for the length behind Al Muheer on soft going, whilst Spanish Bounty, only a neck behind the third goes down the same. If we allow 3lbs for the 2 lengths that Spitfire was behind the fourth horse, this puts him on the 94 level, whilst our old friend Little Pete finds himself back on the 88 mark, on which he languished for so long.

Chapter Four

However this was Little Pete's first try at 6 furs and in view of his form figure of 94 against Piscean at Goodwood, we feel he is entitled to the plus sign to signify that he is probably better than 88 now.

The analysis to be made after every race is obviously a process fraught with difficulties and mis-interpretation, as for every person there can be a different set of figures. As in all human affairs, experience is a major factor and "competing" against experts is never easy. Nevertheless, the attempt has to be made and, over a period of time, guided by experience and assisted by a sound interpretation of the facts contained in the bare result, there is no reason why the amateur should not feel himself or herself confident of having an opinion of their own – an opinion based on a sensible assessment of results.

The simple facts of every result are there to be studied and one soon learns what is important and how much allowance should be made when extended distances are involved. It never pays to have wild flights of fancy in studying the form book and, on balance, it is best to see things as they are. The facts are there for everyone to see and it is always best to use them and avoid assumptions as to what might have been if only......!

It is perfectly permissible to give a horse credit of a pound or so in its rating if it seems to have been desperately unlucky but no more than that. To assume that an "unlucky" third or fourth would have won and assess it accordingly is sheer madness. In such circumstances, and if you are sure that the animal in question was genuinely unlucky, it is safest to take the result as it stands and add a + sign after the rating to remind you that the horse is possibly better than is shown by the bald figure. In much the same fashion, a question mark can be put alongside a rating if there is good cause to doubt its validity. For instance, a horse which consistently runs to within a pound or two of say, 94, finishes a long way behind the winner and would therefore "earn" a rating some 14 lbs below the norm, then one would know that the resultant figure is "not right" and completely out of keeping with the horse's normal form.

In such cases, the author takes no more than 7lbs off the official rating and puts a query mark alongside to show some considerable doubt.

Soft or heavy going is always a bugbear and the elongated differences which often occur can be extremely misleading. Despite what the rules say, a sensible jockey will not drive a horse out when it is obviously beaten or not coping with the ground, so we must not assume that a four lengths beating is what it seems. By their very nature, good class handicaps are usually closely contested affairs and finishes of heads and necks are often par for the course. Any race which ends with a strung out procession of tired horses is a real danger sign for any would-be handicapper and readers are advised to exercise great care in making assessments in such cases.

The reader is also cautioned to be wary of results when more than one or two horses are withdrawn from a meeting and the defection of a large number of intended runners when the going is simply given as "soft" is a sure sign that trainers consider things to be a lot worse than would appear to be the case. Such mass absentees are always due to a change of going beyond what was expected and one can safely assume that the actual results are to be taken with a generous pinch of salt.

CHAPTER FIVE

We will now take a collection of past results together with an analysis showing how the revised ratings were decided. Readers are strongly advised to study these in a critical way as the author makes no claim for infallibility and there is no doubt that the interpretation placed on certain results might well be adrift, although such decision have always been made in what seemed a logical way and of course, completely impartially. No attempt has been made to "cook" the figures to fit future results. It needs hardly to be emphasised that one is dealing with fairly volatile animals and nothing can make a person look a fool quicker than a racehorse. Although a surprisingly large percentage of horses run to their rating time and time again, they are not all so accommodating and even without being downright wilful, circumstances can combine to make horses run below form.

Levy Board Handicap run at Beverley

Race 3336

Class 3		5 furs.	Good to firm		Post race ratings
	Everymanforhimself	4.9.8	90		93
Hd	Strike Up The Band	5.9.9	91		92
1 ¼	Johannes	5.8.12	80		78
Nk	Namir	6.8.8	76		74
Hd	Handsome Cross	7.8.8	76		74
Nk	Fyodor	7.9.13	95		92

Our past ratings were:	Everymanforhimself	86/86/90
	Strike Up The Band	No figure
	Johannes	81
	Namir	No figure
	Handsome Cross	No figure
	Fyodor	93/94

Compared against the official ratings we get:	Johannes	-1
	Everymanforhimself	-
	Fydor	+1

The actual result was a fair reflection of the pre-race ratings with the winner and third being in our top three which, for any sprint handicap is as good as one can expect. Speaking after the event, one could point to the fact that the figures for the winner showed a steady improvement and he was a well backed favourite at 5-2. His recent form too, was better than that of Johannes. However, in the event, the latter may have been slightly unlucky. According to the Raceform report he was hampered at the start and always in the rear. He made headway over a furlong out and stayed on strongly to be nearest at the finish. However, as always, we have to accept the result as it stands and the extended distances were the sort that one expects in a sprint handicap run on good to firm going. There was no sufficiently reliable data to be sure which of the first four had run to their rating and we followed a practice which has been found to work out reasonably well before. A matter of 5lbs was allowed for the distances between the winner and third and divided between the two. This meant that the winner went up 3lbs and the third went down 2lbs. Purists might frown at this but it is probably a good a method as any when it is impossible to decide which of the placed horses has run to its official rating. The remainder were assessed from the third horse.

If It was interesting to see what the official thought about all this and the next Ratings List made it clear that no wholesale amendments were on the cards. Everymanforhimself went up 2lbs, Strike Up The Band and Fyodor stayed on the same marks, whilst Namir and Handsome Cross went down a pound. It was clear that our rough and ready amendments had done no damage. One notices that Fyodor received no concession for being sixth but a No 6 draw is not the best place to be in a Beverley sprint and his performance was almost certainly up to scratch. Suffice to say that our figure for Fyodor reflected what actually happened.

Totescoops Handicap - Newcastle

Race 3489

Class 2		6 furs.	Soft Going		Post race ratings
	Geojimali	6.8.9	80		83
Hd	Pawan	8.9.2	87		89
¾	Damika	10.0	99		99
½	Rising Shadow	7.9.12	97		96
1	Baby Strange	4.9.8	93		90
½	Burning Incense	5.9.3	88		84

Pre-race assessments:

Geojimail	-2
Ingleby Arch	-2
Joseph Henry	-2
Pawan	-
Damika	-
Rising Shadow	-

We could be quite satisfied with the way the pre-race ratings worked out as the first four to finish were in our top six assessments. If one wants to have a bet in these circumstances, the only guide is recent form and Geojimali had not been in the first six in his last three outings, hardly a strong recommendation.   In point of fact, none of the top three rated horses had anything to write home about in the last outing or two and, all in all, although one could say in retrospect that the figures were a reasonable reflection of the result, it was not exactly a triumph.

In order to resolve this result we had the choice of taking any of the first three to have run to their official mark and we finally chose Damika because Raceform spoke very highly of his performance.   So, taking Damika as having run to his official rating of 99 meant that the winner went up 3lbs with the rest being amended accordingly.   In soft going the extended distances were, in fact, very tight and any alterations had to be fairly minimal.   Things were slightly confused here because Pawan, who had been set to carry 9.2 was ridden by a 5lb claimer who put up 4lbs overweight.   The next Ratings List put Geojimali on the 84 mark so we weren't far out. In view of Pawan's good run here, it is worth taking a look at his next race.

Turf TV Handicap at Warwick

Race 3647

Class 3	6 furs.	Good to firm in places	Post race ratings	
	Pawan	8.9.3	83	91
1 ¾	Phantom Whisper	5.9.11	91	93
½	Orpenindeed	5.9.12	92	92
Sh Hd	Hurricane Spirit	4.9.13	93	93
½	Johannes	5.9.0	80	79
Hd	Little Edward	10.10.0	94	93

An amazing price!   After his last race in a Class 2 handicap at Newcastle, worth £18.693 to the winner, after which we gave him a rating of 89, here he was on a rating of 83 with Ann Stokes claiming 5lbs.   This happened because this race was only five days after his valiant effort at Newcastle, so he was able to run off his old mark. Yet the public allowed him to start at 6-1. No wonder Raceform referred to him after the race as "the well-in Pawan". No great surprise either that, after this race, the OH put him up to 90 for the prestigious Scottish Stewards' Cup, where he still finished third. The punters at Warwick were certainly fast asleep!

With only a short head between the third and fourth it was highly probable that they had both run to their official rating so, using them as the benchmark made the final assessments a simple task and, apart from the winner going up 8lbs with us, the changes were minimal.

It was nice to see that Phantom Whisper, who had no chance with Pawan on these terms went on to win next time out at 11-2.

Crown Hotels & Restaurants Sprint Stakes (Handicap) Chepstow

Race 3905

Class 2		6 furs 16 yds	Soft	Post race ratings	
	Phantom Whisper	5.9.9		91	95
2 ½	Millfields Dreams	9.8.8		76	78
2 ¼	Signor Peltro	5.9.4		86	86
2	Edge of Light	3.9.9		97	94
Nk	King's Caprice	7.9.8		90	87
2 ¼	Jake The Snake	7.8.11		79	72

Analysis: Only two of the runners had a pre-race rating:

Phatom Whisper   -2
Signor Peltro   +3

After his second to the well handicapped Pawan at Warwick and 2lb well in at the weights on our figures, Phantom Whisper was not a bad bet at 11-2 and he duly strolled home. The weight carried by Millfield's Dreams was thoroughly confusing. Set to carry 8.8 he was ridden by a

7lb claimer in David Probert, who proceeded to put up no less than 12 lbs overweight. Raceform sagely pointed out that "The handicapper is likely to take a dim view of this career best effort". Oddly enough. in his next race 20 days later, the gelding was on an official mark of 75, a pound less than he was set to do here. It was difficult to make heads or tails of the re-assessments and all we could do, and for no good reason, was to take Signor Peltro as having run to his rating of 86 and use him as the benchmark. On soft going we put Millfields Dreams up 2lb for the 2¼ lengths which separated them, allowed another couple of pounds for the distance between him and the winner, which put Phantom Whisper on the 95 mark. The rest were adjusted accordingly but we had no great confidence that we were right.

However, the OH altered his ratings as follows:

Phatom Whisper	5lb up to 96
Millfields Dreams	Down 1bs to 75
Signor Peltro	Down 1lbs to 85
Edge of Light	Stayed on 97
King's Caprice	Down 2lbs to 88
Jake The Snake	Down 2lbs to 77

Perhaps he was as confused as the rest of us.

In addition to information supplied by the official ratings, compiling one's own handicap figures will also highlight an improving horse and as an illustration of this we will spend a little time analysing a few races in which the filly Crimson Fern was involved. She had started her 4yo career on the All-Weather tracks and when she ran at Kempton in January she was no higher than 55 in the Official Ratings. By the time she first attracted our "official" notice by running in a Class 3 handicap she had already gone through the ranks and was now on the 80 mark. This was clearly a filly on the up and up and it would be interesting to see how she fared against slightly better class sprinters.

Delancey Handicap - Sandown

Race 3680

Class 3		5 furs.	Good to firm		Post race ratings
	Crimson Fern	4.8.12	80		87+
1 ¾	Tabaret	5.9.9	91		93
¾	Osiris Way	6.9.3	85		85
1 ¼	Strike Up The Band	5.9.9	91		88
Hd	Playful	5.8.12	80		77
Nk	Tony The Tap	7.8.13	81		77

As stated above, we had no pre-race figure for Crimson Fern but she had met Osiris Way and Playful in a Class 4 5 furs handicap at Salisbury 19 days before and reference to that race put her on about the 78 mark so the filly didn't have to improve much to show up well here. Our pre-race figures were not very informative as only three runners had a rating with us and these were:

Strike Up The Band -1   Tabaret -   Fantasy Believer -

Races where the runners have clashed before are usually informative as they act to confirm previous figures or otherwise and it was not long before we had racecourse proof that Crimson Fern was continuing to improve as she won well, with the trainer reported to have said afterwards that he was hopeful of landing black type with her if the right race could be found.

Working out the after-race figures was straightforward enough as Osiris Way led within the last furlong and had held on well when challenged by both the winner and second. It seemed safe to take him as the benchmark although this put Strike The Band on a lower figure than we would have liked. It was easy to put Tabaret on the 93 mark, a rise of 2lbs from our earlier figure, whilst taking the actual form as it stands put

Crimson Fern on 87 with a plus sign to remind us that she might be better than that.

There was not long to wait for confirmation of our optimistic view as, 8 days later on an official mark of 88, she came out in a Class 2 handicap at Ascot and won "cosily" according to the Raceform race reader.

Keltbray Cup Handicap - Ascot

Race 3943

Class 2	5 furs.	Good to soft	Post race ratings	
	Crimson Fern	4.9.0	88	94
Nk	Strike Up The Band	4.9.3	91	96
1 ¾	Siren's Gift	4.9.7	95	95
3 ¾	Evens And Odds	4.9.12	100	93?
¾	The Trader	10.9.10	98	91?
1 ½	Matsunosuke	6.9.11	99	92?

Pre-race figures were

as follows:		
	Strike Up The Band	-1
	The Trader	-1
	Siren's Gift	-
	Crimson Fern	+1?
	Mac Gille Eoin	+1

The figure of 99 for The Trader had been set up on April 18 and since then he had run three times down the field, although it was significant that the OH still had him on the 98 mark. He is ten years old though and hardly likely to show much improvement so, on balance, it was probably best to let him run. Our figure for Crimson Fern had a plus mark but the figure was strictly on the form shown and trying to guess the improvement in a filly is asking for trouble. One can only assess a horse on what it has actually done. It was strictly a race to watch. To formulate the new ratings, we took Siren's Gift as having run to her official rating of 95. She is a consistent sort and ran a really good race here. As can be seen, using her 95 as a guide put Strike Up The Band who finished nearly 2 lengths in front of her, went up to 96, with Crimson Fern now up to 94. This was Strike Up The Band's 5lbs increase plus a pound for the head which separated them. The first three were well clear of the rest of the field, so the fourth, fifth and sixth all got a query mark.

In view of the trainer's comments after Race 3943 it was no surprise to see Crimson Fern take her chance in the Group 3 King George Stakes at Goodwood later in the month. She was now on the 94 mark, having risen from her lowly 55 mark at the beginning of the year, a massive increase but well earned. Unfortunately, she had the worst possible draw in the number one berth and was always struggling to get to the leaders.

It was therefore interesting to see a return to her old stamping ground in handicaps and there was not long to wait as she ran at Ascot 9 days later and found herself with her old sparring partners.

Shergar Dash Stakes (Handicap) - Ascot

Race 4840

Class 2		5 furs.	Good	Post race ratings	
	Strike Up The Band	5.9.3	94	99
1 ¼	Fathom Five	4.9.5	96	98
¾	Evens And Odds	4.9.6	97	98
Hd	Dark Missile	5.9.7	98	98
Hd	Crimson Fern	4.9.3	94	93
½	Mac Gille Eoin	4.9.8	99	96

The pre-race ratings:	The Trader	-3?
	Strike Up The Band	-2
	Crimson Fern	-1
	Mac Gille Eoin	-
	Fathom Five	+2
	Evens And Odds	+4

For the reasons given in Race 3943 there could be no confidence in The Trader running to his very early figure and the winner, who had been running very consistently, was marginally top rated at -2. Expert opinion in the shape of the Raceform race reader was that Fathom Five "looks handicapped about right" and as he had chased the winner all the way only to give best in the final furlong, he certainly looked a good guide to the level of the form, so he is left on his official rating of 98. A winning margin of 1¼ lengths meant Strike Up The Band going up 5lbs to a new 99 mark but we could be happy with that in view of his recent for which had shown an upward trend. The placings were very tight and there seemed no reason to make any big changes and this was rather confirmed by the reliable Crimson Fern who seemed to have just about run to her rating.

CHAPTER SIX

Having now gone through an analysis of the results of quite a few sprint handicaps, in conjunction with their pre-race ratings, readers may hopefully have reached the conclusion that sprint handicaps are not nearly so difficult to solve as is generally believed. In the Class 2 and 3 handicaps the level of consistency is astonishingly high and there are quite a large number of stalwarts who produce results like clockwork and can be relied upon to run to their rating almost every time.

However, by their very nature and because of big fields, the major handicaps can throw up results which are not quite in keeping with our figures and often the best we can hope for is that our top half-a-dozen top rated horses will include the winner and perhaps a placed horse.

In the two most prestigious sprint handicaps in the first half of the season are the Ascot Wokingham Stakes and the Goodwood Stewards' Cup and we had somewhat mixed fortunes in these races. Conquest, the 40-1 winner of the Stewards' Cup was somewhat fortuitously top rated with us but we could claim no real credit for it, whilst the Wokingham Stakes was a complete disaster.

Our top rated in the Wokingham fiasco were as follows:

Tombi	-2	25th
Bentong	+1	6th
Intrepid Jack	+1	10th
Machinist	+1	12th
Off The Record	+1	16th
Viking Spirit	+1	18th

In their subsequent races these equine marvels failed to overly distinguish themselves, although Tombi ran a very good second in a

£31155 Heritage handicap at York, Bentong misbehaved himself in two subsequent races, Intrepid Jack won a Group 3, no less, Machinist did well to finish fourth in the Stewards' cup and Off The Record finished fifth in a Group 3.

None of the above was any great compensation but one has to say that, on his next outing, Tombi did his best to make amends for a very disappointing run at Ascot.

Sky Bet Dash (Heritage Handicap) - York

Race 4437

Class 2	6 furs.	Good to firm	Post race ratings	
	Lesson In Humility	3.8.12	96	101
1 ¾	Tombi	4.9.9	102	102
Nk	Express Wish	4.8.12	91	91
½	Efistorm	7.8.8	87	86
Sh Hd	Stevie Gee	4.8.9	88	87
Nse	River Falcon	8.8.13	92	91

The top rated horses were:	Tombi	-2
	Stevie Gee	-1
	River Falcon	-1
	Pawan	-1

The latest figure we had for the winner was back in May when she was a head second to Hamish McGonagall in a Class 3 handicap on an official rating of 87. We set her in at 89 on the strength of that run but here she was running on the 96 mark so it was clear that she had not been eating the bread of idleness since May. In fact, she had won an £11656 Classified Stakes at Doncaster over 6 furlongs and been a neck second in a £14760 listed race over 7 furs at Warwick, the latter on a rating of

96. It was plain that our earlier figure of 89 could be thrown in the waste bin. The official rating of 96 put her in the top four rated but we had no reliable tie up with her non-handicap form. She was the only 3yo in the race but she showed no respect to her elders by staying on strongly for a comfortable win. She is clearly better than handicap class

When the third horse is narrowly beaten for second place, with the winner clear, it is usually safe to assume that it has run up to form and so there was no problem in using Express Wish as the marker here, backed by the fact that it was only a pound away from our own pre-race figure. Working through him put Tombi on an earlier figure of 102 and promoted the winner to 101. The third downwards were very close and the amendments were minimal. Pawan, who finished seventh, didn't have a lot of luck in running but probably set up a figure not far from our best figure of 91. Little things like this help to confirm the general level of the form.

We would like to make a point here about retrospective handicapping, where earlier races are re-rated in the light of subsequent events, particularly when a winner goes on to show great improvement. It is perfectly possible to underestimate the form of a race when not too much is known about the contestants but, in our view, it is unwise to revise one's figures on the strength of an improving horse if the figures one has set for the others fit in with what is solidly known. To upgrade those who have finished behind a winner who goes on to "turn handsprings" is asking for trouble and we would strongly advise against such a practice. When a winner goes on to show marked improvement one simply cannot assume that the runners- up will do likewise. They **might** do, but equally they might not and to work like this is courting disaster, although some handicappers have been known to adopt this practice and are forever going backwards and forwards in the form book, usually to their own confusion.

My advice is to treat each horse as an individual and rate him on what he or she does. It is perfectly true that any horse who goes on to show improved form casts reflected glory on those it has beaten but that is all it does. Form students often say that the form of a race has been made to look better when the winner goes on to win everything bar the Boat Race, but I would urge form students not to alter any horse's rating on the strength of what another horse has done.

I would make exception only in the case of 2yo's when little is known of the level of form, especially in the early part of the season and the level in a race is often decided by the class of horses which have won the race in previous years. In the case of 2yo's this is probably as good a way of establishing some kind of form level, but when one is dealing with experienced handicappers whose ratings are almost set in stone , there is no point in doing the same thing. To be fair, I have absolutely no experience of handicapping 2yo's but the time I have spent with older horses convinces me that the only way to assess a horse's rating is to make a judgment on what it has done on a racecourse.

To make an extreme point, at the risk of driving readers to drink, Reigning Monarch, who beat Crimson Fern at Kempton in January on a mark of 55, the same as Crimson Fern just over a length behind, is still merrily jogging round the all-weather tracks on the same 55 mark whilst our old friend Crimson Fern is breathing the rarefied air of the mid 90's. We can also take a less extreme case of Race 3062 where the first three were:

1	Osiris Way	6.9.13	82
2	Playful	5.9.10	79
3	Crimson Fern	4.9.11	80

Dist: ½ ½

This was not so very long ago on June 15[th,] yet only about two months later, Osiris Way is on the 87 mark, an increase from June of 5 lbs, Playful is on the 80 mark, but Crimson Fern is now on the 94 mark, an increase of 14 lbs, with perhaps more to go. Imagine anyone looking back at this race and, noting that Playful beat Crimson Fern ½ length on near enough the same official rating, takes the view that Playful should also go up 14lbs.

These are fairly laughable examples but then, the whole idea of assessing horses on the strength of what rivals go on to do is also ludicrous and if this book has served to stop any budding handicapper from doing this, it will have been worth the price.

Some years ago *Raceform Update* published a table I had compiled which purported to indicate the average increase in rating which the OH allots according to the winning distance. This was intended to be a rough guide to would-be handicappers and ran as follows;

Below ½ length	4 lbs
¾ length	5 lbs
1 length	5 lbs
1 ½ length	5 lbs
2 lengths	5/6 lbs
2 ½ lengths	5/6 lbs
3 lengths	7lbs
4 lengths	8/9 lbs
5 lengths	10 lbs
6 lengths	10 lbs

These figures were average penalties calculated from a fairly large number of results and were intended to show what increase in rating was likely after any horse had won a race.

Simply as a matter of interest and to those who are often wary of a horse carrying a penalty, it is worth noting that the amount of the penalty if often less than the possible increase when the horse is re-assessed and a winner who is brought out again very quickly is often temporarily better off than it would be in a week or two's time.

To a certain extent, the figures have been overtaken by events and winning distances can be in increments of ¼ lengths and it is quite common for the winning and extended distance to be shown as 1¼ or 2¾ lengths. These new distances serve no really practicable purpose as it is highly probable that the OH imposes the same penalty for winning by 1¼ lengths as if the margin was 1½ lengths. No doubt some bright spark in racing's hierarchy saw fit to impose this kind of mathematical nonsense on the general public. Even worse however, is the very recent decision to introduce the new winning distance of a nose. This has presumably come from the US – a country where the majority of States allow medication whereby the pain barrier for horses is raised and unsound horses win prestigious races they might otherwise have lost.

It would be interesting to hear the powers-that-be explain precisely the difference between a short head and a nose and why it was thought necessary to introduce such a ridiculous margin. It must be heartbreaking for connections to see a gallant horse deprived of a race which, in the good old days, he would at least have shared.

Of course, in these days of political niceties it is possible that it is intended to introduce a new system of penalties which will include half-pounds or even ounces. Should that day ever dawn, as the legendary Sam Goldwyn would have said – include me out.

Fortunately, none of this need concern handicappers – professional or amateur - and the above table can serve as a very rough and ready guide. Winners always get penalised and the amount by which they are punished is largely dependent, not only on the winning margin, but the manner of the win. As far as the latter element is concerned the amateur is greatly assisted by the comments of skilled race readers and the post-race comments printed in the Form Book or in Raceform Update are quite invaluable.

Paying close attention to the opinions of these experts helps greatly in building up a picture in the mind of what actually happened. Did the winner scrape home by the skin of its teeth and could not have pulled out another inch, or was it a very comfortable win with plenty in hand?

The Raceform comments will clearly guide the careful reader and such an aid is of great assistance in making a decision about fresh assessments.

Let us take an example:

Hong Kong Sprint Stakes (Handicap) - Ascot

Race 4445

	Class 2	5 furs.	Good to firm	Post race ratings	
		Tom's Laughter	4.8.7	89	94+
1 ½		Strike Up The Band	5.8.9	92	93
Nk		Total Impact	5.8.0	83	83
Hd		Safari Mischief	5.8.5	88	87
1 ¼		Orpsie Boy	5.8.13	96	93
1 ½		Bertoliver	4.8.12	95	90

The following comments are from the official Form Book:

"Tom's Laughter, dropped back in distance and fitted with blinkers for the first time, showed good speed from his favourable high draw and, racing close to the far-side rail, stayed on strongly to score decisively.......................He has the potential to improve further and could well contest Listed races by the end of the season........."

Strike Up The Band, who has been running well in defeat recently, looked to have plenty in his favour drawn very high. He showed his usual early speed and had every chance, but the winner had him comfortably held at the finish.

No-one reading these incisive comments could fail to appreciate that Tom's Laughter was, in fact, a very easy winner, worth more than the 1½ length verdict. They also make it clear that, well though he ran,

Strike Up The Band could not have pulled out any more even though he was "pushed" for second place by Total Impact who was only a neck behind.

Thus, a clear picture of the finish emerges and, taking Total Impact as the benchmark produced the above ratings. It will be seen that Strike Up The Band is put up a pound for his head in front of Total Impact but, when it comes to assessing the rating for the winner, we have to take the result as it stood and put Tom's Laughter up to a mark 5lbs above his official rating, which was a pound added to Strike Up The Band, plus 4 lbs for the winning margin of 1½ lengths. We could however, give the figure a plus mark to show that he was probably better than the bare figure indicated. The remainder were easy to amend.

Tom's Laughter's next outing could not fail to be of great interest.

De Boer Stakes (Handicap) Goodwood

Race 4555

Class 3	5 furs.	Good to firm	Post race ratings	
	Total Impact	5.9.1	82	86
Nk	Even Bolder	5.8.3	70	73
1	Mandurah	4.8.4	71	71
Nse	Tom's Laughter	4.9.10	91	91
Sh hd	Tony The Tap	7.8.13	80	80
¾	Ocean Blaze	4.9.1	82	80

Tom's Laughter, on a rating only 2lbs higher than at Ascot 4 days previously, was well backed to win this but let Raceform tell the story.

"**Tom's Laughter** was only 2lb higher than when winning a valuable sprint at Ascot four days previously but he got very warm beforehand

and could not confirm form with Total Impact. Official explanation: jockey said gelding was unsuited by the good to firm ground"

The race comment for Tom's Laughter said, "lw. awkward at start but led group towards near side till inside final furlong: one pace near finish"

Leaving aside the jockey Kevin Ghunova's explanation (the going had also been good to firm at Ascot), it seems that, for whatever reasons, the horse was not quite the same animal which strode home so majestically at the Berkshire course just four days before. The rating he achieved here was 3lbs below that achieved at Ascot but there had hardly been enough time for the expected improvement to take place. However, there was no suggestion that the race had come too soon after Ascot so it was just a case of wait and see.

NOTES

CHAPTER SEVEN

It is an unfortunate fact that, in the compilation of a private handicap and using them for the purpose of finding a decent betting opportunity, there is a recurring problem in that, having compared one's ratings against the official figures on a particular day, one finds that some of the ratings in one's records were either recorded some time back or the horse in question has been running several times without earning a figure. This might be due to several factors and, in the case of better class horses, they may run in Listed and Group races, or out of the first six in good handicaps, with the consequence that, though the candidate in question has a very good figure which puts him high in the ratings, doubts creep in due to the foregoing circumstances.

We will examine the following.

Toteswinger Heritage Handicap - Windsor June 28

Race 3504

Class 2		6 furs.	Good to firm		Post race ratings
	Hitchens	3.9.1	102		107
nse	Hoh Hoh Hoh	6.9.6	100		105
1 ¾	Siren's Gift	4.9.1	95		95
nse	Mac Gille Eoin	4.9.6	100		99
Nk	Ashdown Express	9.9.6	100		98
¾	Nota Bene	6.9.10	104		101

Apart from the 1¾ lengths which separated the winner and second, the extended distance show this £31,155 race to be a well contested sprint. In fact, the distance which separated the front two from the rest pointed to their having put up meritorious performances. Mac Gille Eoin had won a Class 2 handicap at Epsom three weeks before, earning a rating with us of 99, which was a pound below that of the Official Handicapper.

It did not seem unreasonable to use our rating of 99 as the marker here and calculate the rest from him. This would put Siren's Gift on 95 which meant that Hoh Hoh Hoh had to go up at least 5lbs for the 1¾ lengths by which he had beaten Siren's Gift and, allowing nothing for the nose win, we put the winner up by the same 5lbs. Ashdown Express and Nota Bene virtually worked out the own ratings.

This clearly put Hoh Hoh Hoh on a figure which made him one of the best sprinters around and a bit better than handicap class. Such horses are difficult to win with as they are weighted out of handicaps and just below the level required to win a Listed or Group race. After the Windsor race he ran in a Listed race at Chester but, not for the first time, he failed to get out of the stalls with any great alacrity and left himself with too much to do. His next appearance was in the Group 3 Hackwood Stakes at Newmarket where he ran quite well, chasing the leader till inside the last three furlongs, but then held out distress signals. As Raceform said at the time, "Hoh Hoh Hoh remains a difficult horse to place". He then came back to handicap company in the Stewards' Cup at Goodwood on a mark of 104 and was up with the leaders for over three furlongs until he cried enough.

This was the situation when he ran in the Class 2 McGee Group Handicap at Sandown at the end of August, except that the handicapper had showed him some mercy and he was on a mark of 100. On his Windsor rating of 105 he was extremely well in at -5, a margin which is very unusual in a handicap with so many rated horses.

Our pre-top ratings were:

Hoh Hoh Hoh	-5	Winner
Dubai Princess	-2?	
Little Edward	-2	Sixth
Fydor	-1	
Little Pete	-1	
Cake	-1	Fifth

Here is the result.

McGee Group Handicap - Sandown

Race 5509

Class 2		5 furs.	Good to Firm		Post race ratings
	Hoh Hoh Hoh	6.9.11	100		105
nse	Crimson Fern	4.9.5	94		99
Hd	Safari Mischief	5.8.13	88		92
½	Matsunosuke	6.9.4	93		96
Nse	Cake	3.9.0	91		94
1	Little Edward	10.9.2	91		91

The fact that our old friend Crimson Fern ran an absolute blinder added to the pleasure when Hoh Hoh Hoh was announced as the winner at 20-1 by the width of a cigarette paper. Speaking after the event it was easy to say that his three outings since Windsor could have been ignored but there remained the fact that, not only was he on a very good rating of -5 in a top class handicap but there was no form book indication that he had definitely deteriorated since Windsor.

En passant, after his win at Windsor, Hitchens ran unplaced on a mark of 107 in a 7furlong Heritage handicap towards the end of July, and 11th on the same level in the Goodwood Stewards' Cup with Hoh Hoh Hoh about 7 lengths behind. After the Goodwood race Raceform commented that Hitchens had a lot to do for a 3yo and we could not argue with that. Constructing the post-race ratings called for care.

It is very rare for a narrow winner to be raised more that three or four pounds in the subsequent official ratings and here one could expect Hoh Hoh Hoh to be put on around the 104 or 105 mark, which is the level at which we placed him after his Windsor race.

If that were to be the case we could re-assess back from the winner by using him as the benchmark. It can be seen that doing this means that the second, third, fourth and fifth horses would go up between 2 and 5 lbs. The question which raised itself was if it were possible that all four horses had improved on their ratings?

One would normally be very wary of this, but there is a theory which holds that, in a bunched finish, horses, being herd animals, will often be "dragged" along by the horses surrounding them in a primal urge for company and, if one accepts that this is possible, the ratings given were perfectly reasonable.

However, in the constant drive to see things as they are, `we referred back to the items about each of the four horses in our database, which gave the following condensed information:

Crimson Fern	87+	94	Gp3	93
Safari Mischief	87	86	86	87
Matsunosuke	92	Stk	4 ?	
Cake	89	92		

For the indefatigable Crimson Fern to go up 5lbs was nothing unusual – she had been doing this all season - and we could live with Safari Mischief showing 5lbs improvement. Matsunosuke had run fourth in a conditions race at Newmarket prior to finishing last in the Hong Kong Sprint at Sandown when his saddle slipped and the gelding might well have improved since earning our rating of 92, whilst Cake's increase was pretty nominal.

On balance therefore, our revised ratings were well within the bounds of acceptability.

There is of course, a need to be satisfied that one's ratings are as truly representative of the actual results as is humanly possible for, apart from highlighting betting opportunities, they reflect upon   future ratings which are influenced by the previous figures.

Analysing the result of any sprint handicap is a fascination exercise of logic and imagination and of course, forms the most important part of compiling a private handicap, so one is well advised to make every effort to get it right. Your data base is most important and needs to be kept as up to date and as comprehensive as possible.

Fortunately, for the most part, the result of a sprint handicap, especially the better class events is very often in line with expectations although it has to be said that getting the winner and perhaps a placed horse in your top four rated horses means you are doing very well. By their very nature, sprint handicaps are very closely contested for, after all is said and done,` the Official Handicapper is aiming at a multiple dead-heat or at least a finish of heads and necks, not to mention noses.

If your judgment is good, and I would stress that this comes from experience, you will usually find that a big plus sign, signifying that the horse has more than the official rating to carry is the kiss of death as far as its chances of winning are concerned. If your data base of ratings is reliable it will be found that most winners have the (-) sign without a number after it, which means it is being asked to do no more than it has done before, or better still, a sign such as -2, which means that the horse has got 2lbs less to carry than it is now being asked to accomplish. The margins are necessarily small, so one aims at establishing a short list from which one hopes the winner will come. Once this short list is made up, the final selection is decided by outside elements such as the going, the draw, course and distance winners and so on but with particular emphasis being placed on a reliable, recent figure.

The data base can be an invaluable source of information if one has a succession of reliable figures for any particular horse, as a rating quite out of kilter with the rest will often indicate that the animal in question was unsuited by the conditions prevailing that day. Every scrap of information is grist to the mill of the private handicapper.

Let us take a race which illustrates how right or how wrong one can be.

Daily Record Garry Own Handicap - Musselburgh

Race 5542

Class 3   5 furs.   Good

Of the thirteen runners there were seven listed with details on our database.

Horse	A&W	Official rating	Database
Ishetoo	4.9.9	92	**96**/89/90/?/90
Fol Hollow	3.9.6	91	**96**/?/?/91/92
Blue Tomato	7.9.4	87	79/Cl4 5/?/?/Cl4 5/**91**/?/?
Princess Ellis	4.9.2	85	**85**/Cl4 3
Geojimail	6.9.0	83	82/**83**/79
Captain Dunne	3.8.12	83	**77**/?/Cl4 2/ Cl4 1
Curtail	5.8.9	78	**80**/?/Cl4 5

N.B. Best rating shown in bold figures

When the best of each horse's ratings is compared with the official figure we get the following:

Pre-race ratings:	Fol Hollow	-5
	Ishetoo	-4
	Blue Tomato	-4
	Curtail	-2
	Princess Ellis	-
	Geojimali	-
	Captain Dunne	+6

Result:	1	Ishetoo
	2	Princess Ellis
	3	Sunrise Safari (No rating)
	4	Sandwith (No rating)
	5	Blue Tomato
	6	Fol Hollow

Although we did not have the winner top rated, our top three were all in the first six to finish. We can take a little credit for having Captain Dunne on a big plus figure for he went on to start the 11-2 co-favourite with the winner and finished 9th.

Working towards a short list is only the first step but, if one's pre-race ratings are reasonably accurate, one is dealing with a small group which, hopefully, will include the winner. As in most races, the winner usually has recent form and by recent we would suggest within the last two or three weeks. As a start therefore, attention should be paid to those horses with a good recent rating. We are looking for a candidate with a minus figure which is to say that his current official rating is below our best rating.

In the above race it seemed sensible to concentrate on the top three in the ratings which were Fol Hollow, Ishetoo and Blue Tomato.

The database details are given above but which we will repeat for clarity's sake.

Fol Hollow	96/?/?/91/92
Ishetoo	96/89/90/?/90
Blue Tomato	79/Cl4 5/?/?/Cl4 5/91/?/?

One is immediately struck by the differences in the respective details, for whereas those for Fol Hollow and Ishetoo are perfectly straightforward, those for Blue Tomato show a veritable witches' brew. Starting off with a low rating of 79, he next ran fifth in a class 4 handicap, followed by two down the field efforts in rateable races. He was again fifth in a class 4 handicap and then somehow earned a figure of 91 when winning a £10,361 class 3 handicap at Hamilton, In view of the fact that the OH put him on a rating of 88, we are inclined to think that we over-rated his performance. Blue Tomato then went on to finish out of the first six in two rateable races. It would not be unfair to venture the opinion that his form is too variable to be a safe bet at any time, which leaves us with Fol Hollow and Ishetoo, both of whom had good, reliable figures.

We will analyse the details for Fol Hollow first and take his last two outings which came after a 96 mark earned in a class 2 handicap at Newmarket in April. In July he ran fifth in a class 3 handicap at Chester for a rating of 91, followed by a fifth in a class 3 handicap at Goodwood (92).

Ishetoo earned his 96 rating when finishing second in a class 2 handicap at Thirsk in May and then finished a good third in the class 2 Scottish Sprint Cup at York (89). He went on to run fifth in a class 3 handicap at Doncaster (90) after which he was slightly out of his depth in the class 2 Gosforth Park Cup at Newcastle, where he finished a respectable 9th with his jockey quoted as saying "he did not get a clear run". His last race prior to this was in a class 3 handicap at York where he finished a very respectable 4th for a rating of 90.

Taking each horse's performance on the whole, it seemed that the form of Ishetoo was of a slightly higher level than that of Fol Hollow so it was no surprise when the former won this race.

Fol Hollow might have been expected to do better than finish sixth but he was one of the only two 3yo's in the race (the other was Captain Dunne) and so could perhaps be forgiven for not being closer to the winner.

It is always wise to remember that you are matching your judgment against that of a highly specialised expert whose working life has the main aim of setting racehorses to compete against each other on equal terms. Of course, they make mistakes and either under-estimate or over-estimate the value of any particular performance. Horses who win by ½ length make it very difficult for the handicapper to judge the worth of the win and one has to bear in mind that no jockey would be thanked by the trainer for winning a decent handicap pulling up by an easy five lengths, for which he will undoubtedly be severely "punished" by a substantial increase in his or her rating.

NOTES

_____

_____

_____

_____

_____

_____

_____

_____

_____

_____

_____

_____

_____

_____

_____

_____

_____

_____

_____

_____

_____

_____

_____

_____

_____

_____

_____

_____

_____

CHAPTER EIGHT

Although the usual practice is to start one's handicapping activities with the start of the turf season in March, one cannot expect too much success too early. The form has to settle down and of course, in assessing any race, it is best to have a firm, reliable rating for as many of the runners as possible. This ideal state off affairs will probably not obtain until about May or June although even then, one gets races where a fair proportion of the runners are having their first race of the season and we have no figure.

It is not really wise to carry figures over from one season to another even though Timeform and other organisations do this but one simply cannot rely on any horse training on and running at the same level as before. It all takes time and a previous year's figures should be taken only as a very rough guide.

Such a race was the Goodwood.Co.Uk Stakes (handicap) run at Goodwood on May 31st when only two of the 8 runners had a rating with us and in both cases were set to carry more than our figure. As a betting proposition the race was a definite no-no but even so, the result carries information for the future and increases our store of knowledge.

Goodwood.Co.Uk Stakes (Handicap) - Goodwood

Race 2598

Class 2	6 furs.	Soft Post		Post race ratings
	Viking Spirit	6.9.10	98	104
2	Pawan	8.8.11	85	87
½	Hurricane Spirit	4.9.6	94	93
Hd	Ebraam	5.9.7	95	93
Hd	Conquest	4.9.11	99	96
Nse	C'Mon You Irons	3.8.2	85	82

The only two of those taking part to have a rating with us were Ebraam (+3) and C'Mon You Irons (+2) so, as far as we were concerned, the race was of academic interest only.

What we couldn't know at the time was that the rating given to Conquest (96) was the figure which made him top-rated for the Goodwood Stewards' Cup but that was after a lot of water had gone under the bridge

With so few horses with a pre-race rating it was difficult to carry out a reliable re-assessment. In such case it is bet to rely on what one already knows (even if only a little) and our previous figure of 93 for Ebraam had seemed firm enough to use him as the benchmark for this race with the rest rated accordingly. The OH gave Viking Spirit a rating of 103 for the Wokingham so we weren't too far adrift.

Things were a bit clearer when the Epsom Derby Meeting came round and the race before the main event was the famous "Dash".

Totesport .Com. "Dash" (Heritage Handicap)

Race 2828

Class 2		Good		Post race ratings
	Holbeck Ghyll	6.8.7	85	89
½	Merlin's Dancer	8.8.5	83	85
½	Safari Mischief	5.8.8	86	86
½	Hogmaneigh	5.9.8	100	98
Nk	Masta Plasta	5.9.8	100	98
Nk	Fathom Five	4.9.5	97	94

Our pre-race assessments were as follows:

Holbeck Ghyll	-1	With the first and third among
Safari Mischief	-1	our top three rated we could feel satisfied things were
Tournedos	-1	taking shape
Canadian Danehill	-	
Bond City	+1	
Masta Plasta	+2	
Northern Empire	+2	

When a race works out well (Even Masta Plasta finished close up fifth), the re-assessments are usual very straightforward, especially when the extended distances are tight. Safari Mischief had been running well and his official rating of 86 was within a pound of our own, so we put him in at 86 with the remainder being simple arithmetic.

Problems often arise with the re-rating of horses when hardly anything is known of the contestants, and when one of the runners in a race has been "turning handsprings" on the all-weather and wins being eased at the finish, it doesn't make things any easier. The effort has to be made of course and one has to hope that things will pan out. Such a case was the following, a minor sprint handicap at Leicester in June.

Arthur Prince Volkswagen, Loughborough Sprint Handicap Leicester

Race 3028

Class 3		Good to soft		Post race ratings
	Befortyfour	3.9.7	95	105
2 ¼	Little Pete	3.8.13	87	88
½	Captain Dunne	3.8.3	77	77
1	Blue Jack	3.8.2	76	74
2 ½	Secret Asset	3.9.5	93	88
¾	Weet A Surprise	3.8.2	76	70

This was not a brilliant race by anyone's standards and we had no figure for any of those taking part. We were aware that Befortyfour had won at Lingfield and the newly built track at Great Leighs but it was difficult to know what the form amounted to.

In passing, the race he won at Lingfield was called the Lingfield Park Derby Trial on May 10 Maiden Stakes, which is as misleading a title as you can get. It is a million miles away from the real thing which attracts near classic types and is over almost 1½ miles.

Although Little Pete had been second and first in two races prior to this event, they had both been class 4 races and had not attracted our attention. There was not a lot to go on but, in words which have become immortal, if you don't know how to do it, ask someone who does. The Official Handicapper is paid to sort these things out and is an expert. According to this highly respected official, Captain Dunne, who ran a good race to finish ½ length behind the second horse, is worth a rating of 77 and this figure is unlikely to be far out, so it seemed not unreasonable to use the gallant Captain as a marker for the purposed of re-assessments. Whilst we could not know this at the time, the Handicapper was thinking along the same lines and, in a race at Haydock 21 days later, he had Captain Dunne unchanged at 77.

One problem remained – how much to put up the winner who was again eased at the finish yet had won by an easy 2¼ lengths? We 'guestimated' 10 lbs, so Befortyfour went up to 105 on our database. As it turned out, he "officially" went up to 103 for his next race at Newmarket , where he was beaten a neck into second place behind Dubai Princess in receipt of 11lbs, with Befortyfour's old Race 3028 playmate, Little Pete, in third place on a rating of 88. The OH obviously thought this was a good performance and when he next ran in a Conditions Stakes at Nottingham, Befortyfour was on the 107 mark. Official Handicappers certainly cast a beady eye on horses who win carefully compiled handicaps, not just by a good margin but easing up into the bargain.

As most readers will know, the draw plays a big part in the results of races at certain tracks where there is often a huge draw bias and at sprint distances, a high or low number can be the kiss of death, depending on the prevailing conditions. It should be noted however, that a bad draw is often pretty well negated by a fast start and even at a circular track like Chester a horse quick on his feet at the start can often overcome the handicap of a bad position in the stalls. Nevertheless, there have been many races where our top of the figures have been drawn out of the race and this can be very frustrating as there is almost no way of estimating how much difference the draw has made to the result.

In race 5109, the Great St Wilfred Handicap won by the David Nicholls' trained Tajneed, that good horse, Knot in Wood, who is one of our personal favourites, had the misfortune to occupy the "coffin box" draw of number one. It is very sad to read the comments of the Raceform race-reader after the race who said, "Knot in Wood had no chance from his draw and might as well have stayed at home" The gelding has also been unlucky in the Goodwood Stewards' Cup where he was well fancied following a cracking win in the Scottish Stewards' Cup at Hamilton (Race 4145).

John Smith's Scottish Stewards' Cup - Hamilton

Race 4145

Class 2		6 furs.	Good to soft		Post race ratings
	Knot in Wood	6.9.7	98		102
Nse	Baby Strange	4.9.2	93		97
2 ¼	Pawan	8.8.13	90		90
¾	Barney McGrew	5.9.3	94		92
1 ¼	Valery Borzov	4.9.3	94		90
½	Maze	3.8.11	93		88

As usual in a race of this description the pre-race assessments were very close:

Pawan	-1	(Third)
Everymanforhimself	-1	
Knot In Wood	-	(First)
Stevie Gee	-	
Rising Shadow	-	
Barney Mc Grew	+1	(Sixth)

In such a prestigious race as this, with a field of 15 good sprinters, one does well to get the winner in the top ratings, so having the first and third in our top four is indicative that one's figures are not too far out, Our equal-top rated horse, Pawan, is a good old stager and as, according to the Raceform representative "he is on top of his game at present" we felt obliged to use him as the benchmark. The going was on the soft side so we can't allow too much for the 2¼ lengths that Baby Strange was in front of him and decided that 4lbs was about right. This put Knot in Wood on the 102 mark and we felt sure he was well up to that mark. The others were amended with due deference to the going.

Baby Strange ran a brilliant race to be beaten a nose by Knot in Wood and, as we had him rated at no higher than 90 prior to this race (he was therefore +3) we felt sure that he was on the up and up. This was confirmed when he again ran a blinder in the Rolf Group Stewards' Sprint Handicap at Goodwood when he was caught on the line by Pearly Wey and beaten a nose, so we were totally amazed when he could do no better than finish 10th in the Great St Wilfred (Race 5109)

Rolf Group Stewards' Sprint Stakes (Handicap) - Goodwood

Race 4586

Class 2	6 furs.	Good to firm		Post race ratings
	Pearly Wey	5.9.10	94	100
Nse	Baby Strange	4.9.9	93	98
1	Joseph Henry	6.9.4	88	90
Hd	Osiris Way	6.9.1	85	86
Nk	Ajigolo	5.9.9	93	93
Nk	Harrison George	3.8.12	86	85

A race with many familiar faces and one where the horses undoubtedly give a nod of recognition to their fellow contestants as they parade. In such a race, it is unusual to get horses with a big "minus" figure so to have two in this handicap was a surprise. The pre-race ratings with us were:

Baby Strange	-4	2nd
Joseph Henry	-4	3rd
Gift Horse	-2	7th
Swinbrook	-2	7th
Dream Theme	-1	9th
Obe Gold	-1	12th

The pre-race figure for the winner was +4 and for Osiris Way --, so, with the exception of Pearly Wey, the race had finished more or less to expectations.   It was in Pearly Wey's favour that he had won this race the previous year and Osiris Way's figure of – meant he was running on the exact rating earned on form.

Baby Strange was due to be raised 4lb for his previous good second in the Hamilton Stewards' Cup (Race 4145) so, as our own figures indicated, he was well in and, as his most recent form was better than that of Joseph Henry, who incidentally was second in this race last year, Baby Strange looked a peach of a bet at 8-1.   Unfortunately for his backers he got caught on the line having led in the last 100 yards.

Apart from the length between second and third it was a tight finish and our feeling was that Ajigolo, who finish very strongly, had run right up to his official rating of 93 and was a candidate as the marker for the re-assessments. The amended ratings put Baby Strange on his highest rating of 98 but this was in keeping with our thoughts after the Scottish Stewards' Cup. Needless to say, we went back to Pearly Wey's previous rating, which had put him on the +4 figure here, to see what had "gone wrong"

We are not in favour of altering ratings by back-tracking" but Pearly Wey's figures called for some investigation.

In the Prince's Stand Stakes (Handicap) run at Epsom on Derby day, Pearly Way, on an official rating of 95, had finished sixth, some 4½ lengths behind the winner, Mac Gille Eoin. In our interpretation of the form we put Pearly Wey on the 90 mark but, in view of his subsequent form, we were plainly adrift, especially as the OH lowered him by just a pound. However, in his next race, the Turf TV Handicap, run over 5 furs at Newmarket, Pearly Wey, on his official rating of 94, could do no better than finish 9th to the winner Sohraab, and beaten the best part of 4 lengths.

In earning a rating with us of 100 in this Goodwood race, Pearly Wey has shown improvement of some 10lbs. We are not inclined to accept this and were prepared to admit that in the Epsom race, we got it wrong.

To confirm this, Pearly Wey's next outing was in a £24,978 Hopeful Stakes, a Listed event run at Newmarket, where he finished a very respectable 6th against some very useful sprinters. Our rating for Epsom had clearly been well adrift.

It always has to be borne in mind that, in our efforts to analyse form, we are, for the most part, dealing with volatile creatures and horses, especially those being prepared for a future race, do not always run up to our own expectations. As the well worn cliché would have it, they are not machines and certainly not governed by numbers in a database.

Anyone attempting the somewhat difficult task of compiling a private handicap has to be prepared for what appear to be setbacks. Sometimes these are due more to mis-judgments than downright error, as it is fatally easy to take a mistaken view about the many close finishes which occur in sprint handicaps. One tries to establish the level of form by taking one, or perhaps two, horses as benchmarks. In the main, this means that one can be on fairly safe ground as past figures act as a guide to accuracy.

If one has a horse which has consistently put up good. reliable figures around the 90 mark, it can be taken for granted that any performance it sets up will be in line with that. Any horse with that kind of record, set up over several weeks, will seldom "find" 7lbs or more and if your figures indicate this sort of "improvement", it is vitally necessary to check against other horses' assessments. Altering one's figures to show that five or six horses in the same race have improved 6/ 7lbs almost certainly means that you have got it wrong. Horses DO improve of course, but this generally happens when its previous form is uncertain or there is only one previous outing upon which to make a judgment. One would certainly not expect this to happen in the case of a seasoned handicapper who has been round the block a few times.

On the other hand, horses certainly run badly below form and there can be many reasons for this. In a sprint, a good start is almost essential and if a horse is badly away and trails the field, the jockey is almost certain to think that there is always another day, with the consequence that one's rating looks wildly adrift. You can nearly always bet good money that the apparent drop in performance is not due to deterioration but just due to the circumstance of the day. Good handicap sprinters run astonishingly consistently up to their mark and any alarming drop in performance is more likely to be due to something physically amiss or an incident in running rather than that one's figures are "up the creek".

One's database will nearly always show if a horse is, in the parlance, going backwards, and any row of figures which show a steady drop in performance nearly always means that the horse has deteriorated and that any early rating should be ignored. Conversely, it a horse's ratings are showing a steady increase, one must always be prepared for an improved performance in excess of what it has already done.

A case in point was the admirable Crimson Fern, whose figures did nothing but improve over a long time. One never knows when a horse has reached its optimum level until a levelling off in performance shows that this is probably the case.

A question which often arises with sprinters is about the interchange from 5 furs to 6 furs, which quite a few seem to do. As a rule they are usually best at one distance or another but there are some who seem equally at home at either. If a sprinter is like Strike Up The Band, who knows only one way to race, which is to jump out of the gate like a bat out of hell, he or she is never likely to stay 6 furs and Dandy Nicholls' charge was only once tried over 6 furs and that was in his first outing in the Cammidge Trophy in which he was patently out of his depth in any case.

A very puzzling case of change of distance was afforded by Thebes, a 3yo colt trained by Mark Johnston. His first four races this year were on the all-weather, of which he won the last three over 6 furs, 7 furs and 6 furs to complete a useful hat trick. The last two races had been handicaps and he raced on a rating of 70 and 76 respectively. The last leg of the hat-trick was on March 22 but, for some reason, he did not appear on a racecourse again until he ran in a handicap at Ascot on June 19, by which time he was on a rating of 88. This race was over a mile and it appeared to the Raceform observer that Thebes did not get the trip,

Mark Johnston apparently thought the same, for the colt's next outing was in a 6 furs handicap over 6 furlongs at Newmarket on the same rating of 88. Still on that mark, he then ran in a 7 furs handicap at Ascot where he led 2 furlongs out, only to weaken quickly and finish 22nd of 25 runners. It was clear he did not stay further than 6 furlongs and he next ran over 6 furs at Ascot on a rating of 84 and which he duly won.

Lloyds TSB Commercial Banking Handicap - Newmarket

Race 5102

Class 2	6 furs.	Good		Post race ratings
	Thebes	3.8.7	84	91
½	Royal Intruder	3.8.13	90	95
2 ½	Wise Melody	3.8.10	87	87
Nk	Tawaash	3.9.7	98	97
½	Always Ready	3.8.4	81	80
1	Marvellous Value	3.9.2	93	92

The pre-race ratings were no guide here:

Wise Melody	-1	3rd
Rubirosa	-1	13th
The Game	--	8th
Rash Judgement	--	9th
Piscean	--	10th

There were no ratings for Thebes or Always Ready and altogether it was bad result for the figures.

It is possible that Mark Johnston, trainer of the winner, was also less than thrilled by a Stewards' Enquiry into the improved form of the winner. Johnston's explanation was that he had no explanation for the apparent improvement in form. Reference to the colt's running since the start of the year seems to suggest that the distance was more to his liking than the 7f and 8 f over which he had been tried. Thebes next ran over 6 f at Goodwood in August but, on a rating of 91, could do no better than finish fifth and, according to Raceform weakened inside the final furlong.

In view of the horse's failures over distances in excess of 6f it was somewhat surprising to see the him take part in the 7.5 f Class 2 Heritage Handicap at Chester later in the month.

He was on an official rating of 91 and ran quite well as he was there with a chance a furlong out but not given a lot of room and could not quicken near the finish. As far as his precise distance requirements were concerned the jury was still out.

In view of the less than spot-on ratings prior to the race it was difficult to assess anything with confidence but, taking the line of least resistance, we took the third, Wise Melody as the benchmark, if only for the reason that she had done best of our top rated horses and it was likely that she had run to her official rating of 87. As it turned out the after-race assessments by the OH were almost exactly in line with ours with the exception of Marvellous Value, who went down only 1lb as against the 3lbs we had knocked off.

This was one of those rather unsatisfactory affairs as far as both the pre-race ratings and the result were concerned, our only consolation being that the Stewards weren't exactly enamoured of it either.

After my previous book, *Sprint Handicapping Explained* was published, many enquiries were received about using race times in connection with the ratings and this called for consideration, as they are used by many racing people to assist in the task of winner finding.

The late Phil Bull, founder of *Timeform* was a great believer in race times and turned them to profitable use. Professional backers like the late Alec Bird obtained his race times from a professional "clocker" and used them to great effect in the backing of 2yo's, often when there was little other guidance as to the value of the form. A 2yo who set up a time that was better than an older horse on the same day and over the same distance could safely be earmarked as a useful animal.

Race times are currently used by many experts in several racing publications and their use is so widespread that their practical use cannot be ignored and one would think that race times would be especially valuable in sprint handicaps where the vast majority of the field is flat out from the start.

The author of this book has nothing against the use of race times in assessing the value of form but feels that a poor time tells you nothing and a fast time is usually confirmed by the actual form of the race as shown by post-race assessments. It is usually the case that a top class sprint handicap, contested by horses, known to be of considerable racing merit in that sphere, will set up a good time, but that tells the would-be handicapper nothing that he or she doesn't already know - that the form is reliable.

There is absolutely no reason why anyone should not use race times as an adjunct to the pre-race ratings if only to confirm the probability of a successful bet, but if a horse is well-in at say, -3, one needs no extra encouragement. The horse is weighted to win so a previous good race figure does no more that increase one's confidence. In our practice, it has never been found necessary to use time figures but this is purely a matter for the individual, although it should be borne in mind that a previous fast time recorded by a prospective candidate in a sprint handicap will avail it nothing if is badly in at the weights.

CHAPTER TEN

Those readers who have progressed this far will by now understand that the most important factors in our endeavours to make sense of sprint handicap results are logic and application. Sprint handicap are, by their very nature, closely contested affairs where the extended distances are very tight and this is a tribute to the work of the OH whose main ambition is to get a multiple dead-heat.

The result of almost every sprint is decided literally by inches and highly dependent on incidents in running. The margins to which all handicappers work are extremely close and even the difference of a pound or two can affect the result. It is therefore vital to be as accurate as possible in the interpretation of any result. Compiling a private handicap of racehorses is like almost every other human endeavour in that practice makes perfect and success attends those who are prepared to work at it.

It necessarily follows that, in order to assess the chances of one horse over others, one has to disagree with the Official Handicapper in the interpretation of results. If it were not so, we would all arrive at the same conclusions and our figures would be precisely the same. It is because we disagree with the OH that we therefore produce pre-race ratings which purport to show that certain horses have less or more weight than allotted.

If our calculations show that one particular animal is set to carry 4lbs less than the official figure this can only be because in one or more of its outings we have considered the performance to be better than was thought by the OH. It might therefore be asked, can the amateur compete with the professional? The answer to this must be in the affirmative because no-one is infallible and, with all his experience and knowledge, the Handicapper can still make mistakes or underestimate the way in which a horse won.

We are involved with a serious sporting hobby where margins are extremely tight but even so, one must not expect mathematical precision all the time. It is wildly optimistic to expect that one's top of the figures will win most of the time. All anyone can reasonably expect is to get the winner in the leading group much of the time. In other words, one uses the pre-race ratings to set up a short list from which one hopes the winner and perhaps a placed horse will come.

It follows then, that it is perfectly possible to have the winner ranked in one's top three most of the time and still fail to back a winner, as the final selection will be based on judgment and a lot of luck. Making the final selection can, however, be very largely a matter of common sense. It usually pays to pay close attention to the candidates which have got good, recent form. As we saw in the case of Hoh Hoh Hoh in race 5509 one should be wary of discarding any horse with a high rating simply because the form is a couple of months old. One has to examine what the horse in question has been doing in the period since it last set up a good figure and to try to ascertain whether the horse has shown any sign of deterioration. If it has run in two or three races since attracting our serious attention in the sense of giving him a rating, seek the advice of the Official Handicapper. If your candidate is currently rated within a pound or two of your last figure it is clear that during the interim it is not considered by a real expert to have suffered any deterioration.

The same logic should be applied to any horse which, on your figures has a big minus figure or, in other words, looks to have a considerable amount in hand. If your last figure is 88, but has run three or four times since then, and is now on an official rating of 80, then my advice is to forget it. Handicappers are very knowledgeable people and it a horse has gone down 8lbs in the space of a couple of months then this is not the sort of animal on which to speculate as it is clear the horse has deteriorated.

If your records show that a horse has set up a good figure but has since run in a variety of different events without earning a figure it is always wise to check with the current official ratings as any discrepancy will indicate the way things are.

Chapter Ten

An ideal situation is one where a horse is a couple of pounds clear on one's own ratings, has shown steady improvement over the last three or four outings, and the official ratings have crept up as well, and in this case, you will almost certainly have an improving horse - the kind that win races. Those animals with figures on a clearly indicated downward trend are best avoided no matter how well in they look. This of course, is why one has to be rigorous in keeping the database up to date as, properly compiled, it will show up or down trends at a glance.

Let us take the case of Bel Cantor, a useful sprinter trained in Wensley, Yorkshire, by WJH Ratcliffe, who won a good £12482 handicap at the end of August. Prior to this race, Bel Cantor was on an official rating of 84 and, having previously set up a figure of 84 with us, he was therefore assessed as ---. Showing he was being asked to do no more than he had done before. Our complete form line for him is set out below.

81 / Cl4 3 / 7fur / 77 / Cl4 5 / Cl4 3 / Cl4 0 / 76 / 81 / 84

The official ratings were:

81 / 80 / 80 / 79 / 79 / 79 / 79 / 79 / 77 / 80 and on a mark of 84 for this race.

Stripped of the "outside" races our actual form figures were

81 / 77 / 76 / 81 / 84

Comparison between the two sets of figures shows a high level of consistency; even though the official ratings took into account races outside our terms of reference.

Ripon Cathedral City Of The Dales Handicap - Ripon August 30th

Race 5503

Class 2   6 furs.   Good to firm in places   Post race ratings

	Bel Cantor	5.8.5	84	91
1 ¾	Swift Princess	4.8.5	84	86
½	Northern Fling	4.9.7	100	100
1 ¼	Joseph Henry	6.8.9	88	85
Hd	Zomerlust	6.8.11	90	85
Nk	Inter Vision	8.9.4	97	92

Pre-race assessments were:

Joseph Henry	--4
Bond City	--1
Stevie Gee	--1
Bel Cantor	--
Northern Fling	--
Barney McGrew	--

We had a previous rating of 86 for High Curragh so, as he was set on the 81 mark, he was "technically" a minus 5 but this is something that has been discussed previously. Since he received that rating High Curragh had run seven times in other events and as he had been downgraded by the handicapper, the early figure was not one upon which to rely. With the first, third and fourth in the shortlist, the result was quite acceptable.

Our highest figure for Joseph Henry was quite a long way back and a more recent rating of 89 was obviously nearer the mark and would have made him −1. He was also one of those whose ratings had gradually gone down since the start of the season − never a good sign.

Chapter Ten

Northern Fling is a very useful horse and looked to have run right up to his rating, so we took him as the marker for the rest. This put Bel Cantor on his highest figure but the OH put him up to 90, which rather confirms the assessments.

NOTES

_____

_____

_____

_____

_____

_____

_____

_____

_____

_____

_____

_____

_____

_____

_____

_____

_____

_____

_____

_____

_____

_____

_____

_____

_____

_____

_____

CHAPTER ELEVEN

Perceptive readers will by now have seen how often the same horses crop up in race after race. In order to "get a mention in dispatches" they have to finish in the first six and it is a tribute to their sheer consistency that we see the same names time after time. This ability to produce their running is a great help to handicappers in general because the placing of just one such animal in the first six is an excellent guide to the level of form and two or three really set the seal on the ratings for that race.

It quite often happens that, by using one reliable horse as the benchmark, and translated down to the rest, it will be found that the third and fourth of the finishers get ratings which are almost exactly what they should be. One can see that, if by using a known rating as a guide to the rest so that the second, third and perhaps the fifth are on their regular level, this will mean that the rating for the winner can be established almost beyond doubt.

This is especially useful in the case of a rapidly improving horse. Many horses suddenly show improved form in a race and the form seems to be more than one would expect, so one is reluctant to put the rating up by say, 8 lbs. If however, the ratings for the horses behind are certain, you have backing for your decision to upgrade a rating by more than the normal amount.

It is when one is dealing with unknown quantities that difficulties arise and, early in the season with no previous form to go by, it is largely a matter of guesswork backed by experience.

There can be a case for almost too much information and the database can contain the records of horses whose career is very varied and hectic. We will take the case of Bel Cantor, who was featured in our most recent race, Race 5503. In which we gave his database form line.

As can be seen his line shows a steady improvement, although some of this has been partially masked by his incursions into a 7 furlongs race and Class 4 races. However, his final figure of 91 is the one of most interest at this time, because it provides an example of what was discussed a few paragraphs back. Bel Cantor's performance in this race was in excess of anything he has done previously this season and one would normally be wary of putting the rating of a seasoned performer up by as much as 7 lbs.

However, as we pointed out, if the rating of those further behind seem to be on their proper mark one has every reason to give the winner due credit for a good win In this case, our slight doubts about the 91 rating were allayed when the OH rating was only a pound behind.

In order further to familiarise readers with this method of form-line we will take that of Malapropism, trained by M Channon. This is rather an extreme case, but illustrates how one can lose track of a horse and be misled by an early rating. Here is the form line.

81 / Cl4 0 / Cl4 0 / Cl4 4 / Cl4 0 / ? / Cl4 6 / Cl4 4 / Cl5 3 / Cl4 4 / Cl5 3 / Cl4 0 / Cl5 2

Malapropism started off with us with rating of 81 (OR 83) but, from then on, ran in races which, apart from one race represented by a question mark, are not rated by us.

The form line gives us no clue to his current standing and, should he run in a Class 3 race, we could not tell if the horse has gone backwards, which admittedly, looks likely or improved. The problem is easily solved, as a glance at his last race shows his current rating is now 73, so he has officially deteriorated by some 10lbs. We would point out that, if we had a horse with an early rating of 81 which had since run twelve times without earning another rating we would ignore the earlier figure, but it is comforting to know where one stands.

Some better class animals often run in Listed or even Group races and their official ratings could well go up, which is something we should know when and if it returns to handicap company.

At the start of Chapter Six, we mentioned the Wokingham Stakes where our pre-race ratings were to prove a disaster. The race resulted as follows;

Wokingham Stakes - Ascot

Race 3248

Class 2		6 furs.	Good to firm		Post race ratings
	Big Timer	4.9.2	100		106
½	Beaver Patrol	6.9.2	100		104
Nse	King's Apostle	4.9.0	98		102
1 ½	Knot In Wood	6.9.0	98		98
¾	Tamagin	5.9.3	101		99
Hd	Capricorn Run	5.9.7	105		103
Dht	Bentong	5.9.5	103		101

In Chapter Six we have explained what happened to our top rated horses subsequent to the Wokingham Stakes but certainly in the Ascot event we were well adrift and it might be of slightly more practical use if we examine the post race ratings.

As always the first task was to find a marker and the one to catch our eye was Knot In Wood, who was drawn on the far side and ran an excellent race. He is a very consistent horse and was unlucky in the draw on several occasions. He finished 1½ lengths behind the equally consistent King's Apostle and putting the latter up from 98 to 102 seemed correct. With Beaver Patrol only a nose in front he goes up 4 lbs as well. This put the winner up 4lbs plus 2lb for the ½ length, making a total increase of 6 lbs. Tamagin, ¾ length behind Knot in Wood, goes down 2lbs, as do Capricorn Run and Bentong, who dead-heated for 6th place.

It was of marginal interest only to see the subsequent official amendments as only Tamagin (100) and Bentong (102) were different.

The Wokingham Stakes is a notoriously difficult race to unravel and the 2008 renewal was well nigh impossible for those who rely on collateral form shown in handicaps. Prior to the Wokingham neither Big Timer nor Beaver Patrol had finished in the first six in a handicap in this country so seeking a line to their form was baying for the moon.

Big Timer's first four races were in Nad Al Sheba:

3rd in the Dubai Trophy (Hdcp) over 1 mile on a –rating of 100

7th in Jazil Stakes (Hdcp) 7.5 furs on 101

8th in Ah Fahidi Gp 2 over 6 furs on 101

2nd in Al Quoz Sprint Listed on 101

2nd in Condition Stakes at Thirsk over 6 fur (Un-rated) *

13th in Duke of York Stakes at York over 6 furs on 101

2nd John of Gaunt Stakes Haydock over 7 furs on 100.

In this race Big Timer finished ½ length in front of Ebraam who was receiving 3lbs and was rated at 99 at that time.

Beaver Patrol had also raced at Nad Al Sheba in his first three races:

3rd in Invasor Stakes (Hdcp) over 6½ furs on 102

3rd in CBD Stakes (Hdcp) over 6 furs on 102

4th in Al Qhoz Sprint Listed on 102

13th in Stan James Handicap over 6 furs at Newmarket on 102

12th Duke of York Stakes over 6 furs at York on 102 *

Chapter Eleven

10th in Gold Star Handicap over 6 furs at Newmarket on 100

In this race Beaver Patrol finished ½ length in front of Big Timer, both carrying 9.7

Those looking for a guide to either of these two horses on a handicap basis were doomed to failure, as about the only guide was Big Timer's having finished just in front of Ebraam, who is a rated sprinter, but non-handicap form is never safely translated to handicap form. Strictly on that run however, Big Timer was obviously on about the right mark at 100, along with Beaver Patrol. That they finished up first and second in one of the most prestigious handicap sprints in this country was putting the boot into those who rely on solid handicap form.

NOTES

_____

_____

_____

_____

_____

_____

_____

_____

_____

_____

_____

_____

_____

_____

_____

_____

_____

_____

_____

_____

_____

_____

_____

_____

_____

_____

_____

_____

It takes quite a few weeks from the start of the turf season in March before an informative database can be built up and it is not usually until about June that one can expect to have a firm figure for most of the runners in a handicap sprint. The Scottish Sprint Cup run at York on May 31st was just such an event and our pre-race ratings were as follows:

Ishetoo	-3
Fantasy Explorer	-2
Masta Plasta	--
Everymandforhimself	+1
Machinist	+1

As it happens, these top five rated horses contained the first, second, third, seventh and eighth which, being fairly early in the season was some evidence that our ratings, at least for the better class animals, were on the mark.

National Express Scottish Sprint Cup (Heritage Handicap) - York

Race 2626

Class 2   5 furs.   Good (Good to firm in places) Post race ratings

	Masta Plasta	5.9.4	96	99
1	Everymanforhimself	4.8.9	87	87
1 ¼	Ishetoo	4.9.1	93	89
Nse	Tabaret	5.8.9	87	83
1	Siren's Gift	4.9.3	95	89
Hd	Indian Trail	8.9.10	102	97

The trainer of the winner, Dandy Nicholls, often referred to as the sprint king, usually sets his own puzzle by having multiple runners in these valuable sprints and the fact that his son Adrian rides one of the runners is not necessarily indicative that it is the stable selected. Whether or not the market is any guide is also open to doubt but, in this case, the shortest of the Nicholls' four was Machinist at 8-1. Masta Plasta had worn a visor when, ridden by Adrian Nicholls, he had finished third to his stablemate Manzila, a French import, ridden by Silvestre De Silva. For this race, the visor was left off and Masta Plasta had the services of a 7lb claimer, Adele Rothery, with Adrian Nicholls among the also-rans on Northern Fling.

Whilst one has to accept that trainers are in the best position to know the present well being of their charges, we have found that, if television pre-race interviews are any guide, they are seemingly as much in the dark as the punter where multiple runners are concerned. For our part, we can only say that, on our figures, Masta Plasta was the best of the Nicholls' four and in all such cases, our readers are advised to be guided by what their ratings say and to ignore outside influences.

For the re-assessments we took Everymanforhimself as the one to rely on for the standard. He had run a good race last time out and here had run his heart out when chasing the winner all the way. It seemed abundantly clear that he had run right up to his official rating. We gave Masta Plasta the full 3lbs for the length by which he had won and allowed Ishetoo 4lbs for the 1¼ lengths he was behind the second. The rest were straightforward enough.

Another June race which attracted our attention was a £15,577 event at Epsom, the fastest course in the country.

Prince's Stand Stakes (Handicap) - Epsom

Race 2831

Class 2	6 furs.	Good		Post race ratings
	Mac Gille Eoin	4.9.5	93	101
1 ½	Our Faye	5.8.8	82	86
1 ½	Gift Horse	8.8.11	85	85
Hd	Sweet Pickle	7.8.6	80	79
½	Idle Power	10.8.10	84	81
1	Pearly Wey	5.9.7	9590	83?

Our pre-race assessments were:	Pawan	-3
	Joseph Henry	--
	Machinist	--

This was typical of an "early" race as far as ratings went, as these three were the only ones with a rating out of the twelve runners. It is hardly ever wise to have any financial interest in a race with so many unknown quantities and Pawan, despite his -3 is hardly the most prolific winner of all time. The main value to be obtained from the race were the post race ratings, but these were not easy. We studied the post-race comments very closely and it certainly seemed that Gift Horse, trained by Dandy Nicholls, had run on very well and had snatched third place on the line. It was a fair assumption that he had run up to his official rating and was therefore taken as the benchmark. The first three were a bit strung out for a handicap sprint and we decided to allow 4lbs for the 1½ lengths between them as shown. We found subsequently that the OH had left Gift Horse on the same rating of 85. The fourth, fifth and sixth were amended as shown. Pearly Way only went down a pound in the official ratings but it is not to be expected that a horse placed no nearer than sixth will go down 5 lbs on the strength of one race. We have the freedom to do that, and can represent the actual form. A rather more productive race was the following:

Poker at Bet365 Handicap - Haydock

Race 3723

				Post race ratings
Class 3	6 furs.	Soft		
	Great Charm	3.9.2	83	90
¾	Dunn'o	3.8.13	80	85
2 ¼	Errigal Lad	3.8.11	78	78
Hd	Honey Monster	3.9.4	85	84
1 ½	Baldemar	3.9.7	88	85
Nk	Marvellous Value	3.9.7	88	85

The pre-race assessments were:

Great Charm	+4
Irving Place	-1?
Solar Spirit	--
Captain Dunne	--
Baldemar	+1

(Dunn'o and Errigal Lad had no rating)

At 15-2 , Great Charm, who had been in good form and had won on soft going earlier was a good price and led all the way, doing enough to hold on for a useful win.

During the course of a season the amateur handicapper often suffers a temporary reverse when a reliable looking shortlist of candidates is found not to include the winner. We will consider the following example.

John Smith's Extra Cold Stakes (Handicap) - York

Race 3973

Class 3	6 furs.	Heavy		Post race ratings
	Zomerlust	5.9.5	85	87
1`	Kaldoun Kingdom	3.9.3	89	89
½	Swift Princess	4.9.3	83	81
1	Ishetoo	4.9.13	93	90
½	Bel Cantor	5.8.13	79	76
2 ¾	Baby Strange	4.9.13	93	88?

Top rated list:	Ishetoo	-3
	Bel Cantor	-2
	Kaldoun Kingdom	--
	Swift Princess	--
	Baby Strange	--

As can be seen, all the above candidates finished in the first six, but were eclipsed by a horse who, in his previous four outings this season, had been exhibiting all the signs of paralysing inertia. His four outings revealed the following:

13/17	In Class 2 handicap on soft going at Doncaster
11/12	In Class 2 handicap on g/soft going at Pontefract
15/15	In Class 2 handicap on good/firm going at York
8/4	In Class 2 handicap on soft going at Newcastle

Only in the most recent of these outings did Zomerlust show any inclination to be competitive and the perceptive post race comments of the Raceform race reader after this race read:

" Zomerlust, who has slipped in the weights, had conditions to suit and ran as though better than the bare form after finishing clear of those on the unfavoured side. A strongly run race over either this trip (7 furs) or over 6 furs suits and he is one to keep an eye on"

He had won a similar event in soft going almost a year ago, so his return to form here was probably not such a total surprise to his connections as it seemed at the time for he started 4-1 favourite. He is reputed to be a lazy individual and Robert Winston had to be at his strongest to keep the gelding up with the leaders, as a result of which he picked up a two day whip ban.

From our admittedly biased point of view the race had an unsatisfactory result as Zomerlust had not finished in the first six at any time this season and we thus had no figure for him. Nevertheless, with five top rated horses in the first six, we could claim a partial success. To resolve this, we took Kaldoun Kingdom as having run to his official rating. He is suited by the ground and, after taking the lead in the final furlong, he was overtaken by the winner who stayed on well in the last 100 yards. In heavy going the amendments have to be minimal and we give Baby Strange a query as, according to the jockey, "he ran too free" and was never going to see it out. It has to be said that Zomerlust did not impress in three subsequent outings, one in heavy going, so is not perhaps one to be entrusted with too much of the betting bank.

The next race we deal with has fortunately got no skeletons in the cupboard and everything work out quite well.

Armstrong Memorial Handicap - Ripon

Race 4687

Class 3		6 furs.		Good		Post race ratings
	Bond City		6.9.2	86		90
¾	Harbour Blues		3.8.10	84		86
¾	Grazeon Gold Blend		5.8.8	78		78
1 ¾	Great Charm		3.9.1	89		86
1 ½	Prior Warning		4.9.11	95		90
Hd	Geojimali		6.9.0	84		79

The pre-race ratings:	Ajigolo	-2
	Bond City	-1
	Great Charm	-1
	Prior Warning	-1
	Grazeon Gold Blend	--
	Geojimali	+1

As the draw at Ripon can often be of great importance in sprints, it is interesting to note the Raceform comment that, in the preceding 5f seller, those drawn on the far side (high) were at a huge advantage but in this smaller field there seemed to be no bias.

The top rated Ajigolo, failed to give his running and, as Raceform had it, "was rather disappointing".   He was either not in the same form as when running so well in Race 4586 (Chapter 8), or there was something amiss.   Great Charm, who had done us a good turn in Race 3723, had gone up 6lbs in the official ratings but, in the meantime had run a good race when close up fifth to Spanish Bounty in a £62,310 Heritage Handicap at Newmarket and was still on a good mark with us, although he probably needs a slightly easier surface.

Although not in the right order, five in the top six to finish is as good as one can reasonably expect. We had no figure for Harbour Blues but he had been doing quite well in lower class handicaps or on the all-weather.

Resolving this result was done by taking Grazeon Gold Blend as having run to form and he had two figures of 76 and 78 to his credit. The rest were amended according to their placings and extended distances which put Bond City on the 90 mark. The OH agreed, but the gelding made no show in two subsequent races on that level.

Mention of Great Charm's good showing in Race 3850 takes us to an analysis of that race.

Toteswinger Stakes (Heritage Handicap)

Race 3850

Class 2		6 furs.	Good to soft	Post race ratings	
	Spanish Bounty	3.8.7		90	93
¾	Spitfire	3.8.12		95	96
¾	Tawaash	3.9.0		97	96
Hd	Dohasa	3.9.7		104	102
Nse	Royal Intruder	3.8.7		90	88
1 ½	Wigram's Turn	3.8.3		86	81

Pre-race ratings:	Spanish Bounty	-1
	Great Charm	-1
	Wise Melody	-1
	Carleton	+1

The value of the ratings was shown, here although only one of our top four earned a place! Great Charm finished 7th, Wise Melody finished last, but the ground was not now in her favour and Carleton finished in

15th place. However, these were completely overshadowed by Spanish Bounty's magnificent win at 33-1. He was certainly over-priced as he had good form coming into the race and had a rating of 91 in Race 2967. One of the surprises of the race was the forward showing of Spitfire, who was +4 with us but Frankie Dettori's estimable presence on his back was probably worth a pound or two.

With several un-rated (with us) horses concerned in the finish we adopted a somewhat unorthodox procedure, which has worked in the past. The distance between the first and fifth was a fraction under 2 lengths and we allowed 5 lbs for this, put the winner up 3lbs of this and knocked the other 2 lbs off Royal Intruder, with the rest in rough proportion.

With such a close finish it is never going to be far out.

NOTES

_____

_____

_____

_____

_____

_____

_____

_____

_____

_____

_____

_____

_____

_____

_____

_____

_____

_____

_____

_____

_____

_____

_____

_____

_____

_____

_____

_____

CHAPTER THIRTEEN

At this stage, and from the point of view of assisting those readers who are still uncertain about the re-assessments, we will go back to some of the earlier races of 2008. In these races there were obviously no pre-race ratings, so we will pay more attention to the amendments made to the official ratings in the light of the result. The analysis which attends each race explains how the re-assessments have been worked out but we would emphasis that these are purely a matter of opinion and readers are quite free to disagree with our findings. Whilst this book is not intended to be an instruction manual it is hoped that those interested will find the analysis of races to be of guidance when they compile their own figures.

We take this early race as a good example.

Urban-I-Handicap - Doncaster

Race 1325

Class 2	5 furs.	Soft		Post race ratings
	Northern Fling	4.9.4	96	99
½	Chief Editor	4.8.13	91	92
¾	River Falcon	8.9.1	93	93
1 ¾	Green Park	5.8.11	89	86?
2	Bond City	6.9.2	94	89
Sh hd	Fantasy Believer	10.8.13	91	86

There is little to guide us in a race where most, if not all, are having their first race of the season. We need all the help we can get and the official ratings are probably the best guide to the standing of the race. The ratings are the work of an expert and so we take them as a starting point. However, the result itself "proves" that these initial assessments need some fine tuning, as it is self evident that not all the horses have run to their rating.

But where to start? With no form to guide us and, since we cannot see into the future, the next best way to resolve the problem is to consult the Raceform comments, which are always a good guide. Their judgment as to whether a horse has run up to its rating is invariably excellent. In the above race the after=race comments in Raceform contained this comment about the third horse.

"River Falcon, just 1lbs higher than when winning at York last August, stepped up on the form he showed over 6 f here on his re-appearance and this was a solid effort"

This sounds a reasonable recommendation and as the race comment said that "he kept on under pressure" it certainly confirms that he had run to his rating and to use him as the benchmark seemed sensible. We give Green Park a question mark with his new assessment because , according to Raceform, "he did not have much room when trying to make his move and would probably have finished a length or two closer with a better run". These are very valuable comments to read to enable one to get an overall picture of what happened in the race.

It is interesting to compare our new ratings against those of the OH.

	Self	OH
Northern Fling	99	103
Bond City	89	92
River Falcon	93	94
Green Park	86	88
Chief Editor	92	94
Fantasy Believer	86	89

Chapter Thirteen

It would appear from these figures that the OH took a slightly more elevated view of the form of the race than we did, with the winner going up a hefty 7lbs, which seemed quite harsh for a ½ length win on soft going.

In mitigation, it is not perhaps out of order to mention that that, with the exception of Chief Editor, who won next time out, they all ran a considerable number of times without winning . The future outings of Northern Fling (6 times), River Falcon (5), Green Park (7), Bond City (8) and Fantasy Believer (6) tend to support the belief that they might possibly have been slightly overtaxed.

We will continue our analyses of races with the following:

Dubai Duty Free Full of Surprises Handicap - Newbury

Race 1442

Class 2	5 furs 34 yds	Good to soft	Post race ratings	
	Oldjoesaid	4.9.4	102	105
Nk	The Trader	10.8.13	97	99
1	Fullanby	6.9.3	101	101
¾	King Orchisios	5.8.12	96	95
3 ¼	Hogmaneigh	5.9.4	102	97?
4	Elhamri	4.8.6	90	83?

This was another race where the Raceform post-race comments were useful in deciding which horse/s to use for guidance. The comments about Fullanby ("...this was a good start") and King Orchisios, ("...could just keep on one pace when headed") were useful hints that they had run to their best and Fullanby's rating of 101 was used as the main guide to the rest.

Again, it is of interest to compare the revised assessments:

	Self	**OH**
Oldjoesaid	105	107
The Trader	99	100
Fullanby	101	101
King Orchisios	95	95
Hogmaneigh	97?	101
Elhamri	83?	88

Due to the soft going and the somewhat extended distances between the fourth and fifth and fifth and sixth, our assessments for Hogmaneigh and Elhamri were considerably at variance with those of the OH ,but it has to be borne in mind that, come what may, the official is very unlikely to lower the rating of any horse more than a pound or two. He is inhibited by the demands of the situation, whereas we can do what we like and knock off 5-7 lbs at will.   Sadly, poor King Orchisios was to die in his next race.

In the next race under examination, there were only four horses with a reliable rating but even so, they were a good guide, if not for betting purposes, but to show the figures one has already built up are working out.

Chapter Thirteen

RIU Palace Meloneras Handicap - Pontefract

Race 1517

Class 2	6 furs.		Good to soft		Post race ratings
	Turnkey	6.8.8	90		93
Hd	Damika	5.8.13	95		97
Hd	Stevie Gee	4.8.4	86		87
¾	Genki	4.9.3	99		99
¾	Ingleby Arch	5.8.7	89		87
1 ¼	Distinctly Game	6.8.4	86		81

Our pre-race assessments

were as follows:

Turnkey	-1
Damika	-1
High Curragh	--
Ingleby Arch	+5

Those who question the importance of just a pound or two would do well to look at the performance of the first two in this race. In their last outing they had finished 6th and fourth respectively behind Cape in a 6 furlong handicap at Doncaster. On that occasion Turnkey had been on an official rating of 91 and finished a neck and a head behind Damika on a rating of 95. After that race, Turnkey was allowed a pound for the beating on good to soft going so things were bound to be close. Our figures showed them on the same level of -1 and there was just a head between them at the finish when Damika was just headed on the line. The fourth horse Genki, was driven into the lead well inside the final furlong only to be headed inside the last 50 yards. He had obviously run his heart out and made a good choice as the benchmark horse so was left on his official rating of 99.

With such a blanket finish, the calculations for the rest were quite simple as shown.

A comparison between our assessments and those of the OH shows only a minimal difference but we were rather more lenient towards the fifth and sixth.

	Self	**OH**
Turnkey	93	93
Damika	97	97
Stevie Gee	87	86
Genki	99	99
Ingleby Arch	87	89
Distinctly Game	81	84

In our next race for analysis there were again just four horses with a rating with the result as shown below.

Betfredcasino Handicap - Haydock

Race 2401

Class 2	5 furs.	Good to firm		Post race ratings
	Fyodor	7.8.11	92	94
Nse	Intrepid Jack	6.9.7	102	104
1	Invisible Force	4.8.9	90	90
2	Northern Fling	4.9.8	90	90
Nk	Knot In Wood	6.9.4	99	96
Nk	Green Manalishi	7.9.9	104	101

Pre-race assessments:	Fyodor	-1
	Bond City	+1
	Invisible Force	+4
	Northern Fling	+4

Bond City, who is better on a softer surface, was the only one on the shortlist to finish out of the first four, so it was a good result for the figures. Fyodor doesn't win very often but the first time visor might have made all the difference here , as he held on very gamely in the last few strides, aided by jockey Michael Hills, who is one of the best in the business.

Our post-race ratings were centred round the official rating of Invisible Force, who ran a good race only to be headed well inside the final furlong.

The comparison again shows that, in a close finish, the re-assessments can never be more than minimal,

	Self	**OH**
Fyodor	94	96
Intrepid Jack	104	105
Invisible Force	90	89
Northern Fling	100	102
Knot In Wood	96	98
Green Manalishi	101	103

From these figures one can see that the OH had set the level of the race slightly higher.

When compiling one's own private ratings it is always encouraging if the results bear more than a passing resemblance to the pre-race figures and of course, a good priced winner is the icing on the cake. We have to admit however, that 25-1 winners are not an every day happening and the result of the following race, whilst not a total shock, came as a bit of a surprise.

Goldstar Transport Handicap - Newmarket

Race 2426

Class 2		6 furs.	Good	Post race ratings	
	Ajigolo	5.8.4	86	90
1 ¾	Express Wish	4.8.7	89	90
½	Everymanforhimself	4.8.5	87	86
¾	Baby Strange	4.8.11	93	90
Sh hd	Prior Warning	4.9.3	99	96
Sh hd	Cape	5.8.10	92	89

Pre-race assessments:	Ajigolo	-3?
	Everymanforhimself	--
	Cape	--
	Phantom Whisper	+2
	Pusey Street Lady	+2
	Dream Theme	+2

With three of our top ratings finishing in the first six, including the 25-1 winner, there was perhaps some cause for celebration except for one small snag – the dreaded question mark against the assessment of Ajigolo.

Any horse which is top on one's figures needs more than a cursory look, but Ajigolo's recent form was not exactly encouraging. We had given him a rating of 89 when last of five over nearly 6 furs at Brighton midway through April ,but he was patently not suited by the track and was eased in the final furlong to finish some way behind the winner. The figure had to be doubtful, hence the question mark. After that debacle, he was 5/7 at Yarmouth, 8/14 at Chester and, on his most recent outing was 6/12 behind Baby Strange over 6 f at Newbury. He was now 7lbs better off with Baby Strange for the almost ten lengths which separated them in that race, and that didn't look enough.

Whilst using pre-race assessments to set up a short list for the race, common sense is also called for and Ajigolo did not look the kind of prospect that one would like. The only consolation after the race was that the figures were "right", even if this wasn't reflected in the betting balance.

In re-assessing this race we took the view that 7lbs was about right for the distance which separated the first and third and we took a pound off the official rating of Everymanforhimself and added 6lbs to that of the winner. The rest were done in proportions which readers can easily check for themselves. It is all good practice. As a comment on the OH's amendments after this race, it is sufficient to say that he took much the same view about the winner, who went up to 93 with the remainder virtually unchanged, with the second going up 2lbs.

It is necessary to point out that one's figures rely heavily on judgment and it has to be said that there have been occasions when events have proved that one is far from infallible. It is often somewhat unsafe to assess the rating of a winner when the resultant rating is well in excess of anything it has done before. We will quote the case of the Dandy Nicholls' trained Blue Tomato, and show a race he won where we appear to have badly misjudged the value of the win.

Clyde 1 One Thousand Pound Song Handicap - Hamilton

Race 2938

Class 3	6 furs.	Good to firm		Post race ratings
	Blue Tomato	7.9.5	83	91
½	My Gaucho	6.8.9	73	79
2 ½	Rainbow Fox	4.8.4	68	68
1	Yorkshire Blue	9.8.4	68	65
Nk	Avertuoso	4.9.3	81	78
1 ¼	Curtail	5.9.7	85	80

For reasons which probably seemed valid at the time, this race was re-assessed by using the third horse, Rainbow Fox as the benchmark and this resulted in Blue Tomato being given a rating of 91. We should have realised that something was amiss with this, as it put Blue Tomato on a figure 12lbs higher than anything he had done before and it was extremely unlikely that he had improved that much. He had recently been running in Class 4 and Class five handicaps without setting the world alight. In such case, it is advisable to check one's assessment with that of the OH and this would have shown that he had given it a rating of 88. Unfortunately, a mis-cue of this kind has repercussions and when Blue Tomato next ran, his high rating (with us) gave a reading of -3, which of course, gave him an excellent chance. We show this race for further explanation.

TurfTV Handicap - Newmarket

Race 4201

Class 3	5 furs.	Good to firm	Post race ratings	
	Sohraab	4.9.12	93	98
Nk	Ocean Blaze	4.8.13	80	84
½	Tony The Tap	7.8.12	79	81
¾	Misaro	7.9.9	90	90
Sh hd	Osiris Way	6.9.4	85	85
Nk	Golden Dixie	9.9.4	85	83

Pre-race ratings:	Blue Tomato	-3
	Golden Dixie	-2
	Sohraab	-1
	Osiris Way	--

All on the shortlist were concerned in the finish except Blue Tomato and there were two possible explanations for this. Either the horse had run well below form, or our previous rating was wrong. As it happens, Nicholls's horse missed the break, is probably better at 6f and probably did quite well to finish 7[th,] only ½ length behind Golden Dixie. Nevertheless, we do not like horses with a pre-race assessment of -3 to finish out of the first six and we had to accept that we were in error. We had overestimated the standard of Blue Tomato's earlier race and the OH rating would have put us on the right lines. An object lesson, which tends to show that one should be very wary of lifting a moderate horse so much in winning a quite ordinary race. However, as the old cliché would have it – you can't win 'em all.

NOTES

CHAPTER FOURTEEN

In these days of political correctness the word "class" has a somewhat sensitive connotation and the terms "lower class" and "upper class" are seldom used.

In the world of racing however, "class" as applied to racehorses, has a clear and definite meaning. It is widely accepted that a top class horse is something special , with the very best of them being called "classic types" and refer to that rare breed capable of holding their own in the very best of races known as Group races.

In our specialised sphere of handicap sprints there are clear distinctions, with handicaps ranging from Class 1 to Class 6 with the lowest performers being in Class 6. There are few Class 1 handicaps and the top handicap sprinters run in either Class 2 or Class 3 events. In this book the only races analysed are in those categories and there is often an overlap between the two, with horses going from one to the other during the course of a season.

Handicap races are also defined as being 0-60, 0-70 and so on up to 0-110. These distinctions are for the benefit of trainers and others who wish to enter their horses in handicap events. A horse officially rated at say 95, would not be eligible to run in a race termed 0-70 but, must keep to its own class and run in races which cater for horses of

his rating. A very lowly rated horse is allowed to enter for a high rated race but would often not get a run because it would almost certainly be weighted well below the minimum weight set for that particular race. If an extremely moderate horse was set to carry 5.13 in a race where the minimum weight was 8 stone, it would, if not balloted out, have to carry an excessive amount of overweight. To do so is often a risky procedure for the connection as, if the horse runs above itself and runs into a place carrying something like 14 lbs overweight (i.e. 14lbs more than the weight it was originally set to carry) the OH would take a very jaundiced view of such a performance and the poor animal's handicap rating would be well and truly clobbered.`

If readers would kindly turn back to the last race analysed (Race 4201), this race carried the annotation (0-95,94) which indicates that the race was for those rated at 95 or less and that 94 was the rating of the highest rated horse taking part. This was Pearly Way who was on the 94 mark and thus carried top weight, which in this case was 9.13.

It will be realised that the official allocation of a very high rating to a horse which has put up a sparkling performance in a decent race, can have serious implications for the connections, quite apart from the pleasure of knowing they have a good horse on their hands. At a certain level, it can become very difficult to place such a horse, for they are too good to run in handicaps and not quite good enough to do more than just about hold their own in Group races. Occasionally, in compiling one's assessments, one has to deal with horses who are top handicap class but whose owners and trainers like to tilt at windmills and take their chances in a non-handicap, Listed or even a Group race.

Such a case is provided by the record of that good sprinter Hoh Hoh Hoh, whose appearances on the racecourse have produced the following.

Race 959   Last in the Listed Cammidge Trophy over 6 furs.

Race 1157   Second in a Conditions Stakes event over 5 furs.

Race 1831   Sixth in the Gp3 Palace House Stakes over 5 furs.

Race 1986   Sixth in a Conditions Stakes over 6 furs.

Race 3504   Second in a Class 2 handicap (0-105) over 6 furs.

(This was his first run in a handicap in 2008 and his prominent placing enabled us to get a handle on his form and assess him at 105)

Race 3948   Seventh in a Class One Listed race over 5 furs.

Race 4188   Eighth in the Gp3 Hackwood Stakes over 6 furs.

Race 4624   Twenty-first in the Class 2 Goodwood Stewards' Cup over 6 furs on a rating of 104.

It can clearly be seen that Hoh Hoh Hoh is capable of more than holding his own in top handicap company but at near level weights in Listed or Group company he is found wanting.

In this book we are dealing specifically with Class 2 and 3 handicaps, but these are occasionally contested by horses which have been running well in lower grade races and are thought to have earned a step up the ladder.

It follows therefore, that in compiling our pre-race assessments, we will inevitably come across one or more of the runners who are "unknown" to us in the sense that they have either not finished in the first six of a Class 2 or 3 handicap or have been running in Class 4 or lower class races This presents us with a problem as we will have no previous rating to guide us in establishing an assessment for the race in question.

Collateral form is sometimes a part-answer as the "unknown" horse may have run against horses in a Class 4 race which have an established rating with us through their participation in a Class 2 or 3 handicap, and it is thus possible to get some idea as to the racing merit of the intruder. It is often not very satisfactory to obtain a second-hand rating in this way and if the unknown, by virtue of good form in lower class races looks to have a good chance of beating the known candidates it is often best to leave the race alone.

Such a race was the following:

Dunnhumby Essential Customer Genius Handicap - Windsor

Race 4928

		Class 3	6 furs.	Good to soft	Post race ratings	
		Mullein	3.8.6	77		82
2		Osiris Way	6.9.5	86		89
1 ¼		Diriculous	4.9.7	88		87

Nse	Kelamon	4.8.6	73	72
1	Idle Power	10.9.3	84	82
1 ¼	Orpenindeed	5.9.10	91	87

Although this race was well into the season (August) most of the runners had not swum into our orbit and we had somewhat doubtful figures for the rest. It was not a race in which to have any financial interest and in any case, was further complicated by the inclusion of Mullein, who appeared to have quite good form in lower class handicaps but for whom we obviously had no figure. Her last outing was when she finished a head second in a Class 4 handicap at Haydock. Unfortunately, none of the other twelve runners in the race had been placed in the first six in a Class 2 or 3 handicap and we therefore could get no line to the form.

All that could come out of the race was further information for the databank.

Osiris Way is a consistent sort and we were prepared to put him up to 89 and take him as a guide to the rest although the resulting figures didn't fill us with the greatest confidence although Osiris Way went on to win a race when top of the figures. (Race 5270 Chapter3)

CHAPTER FIFTEEN

Sprint handicaps often attract a lot of runners, particularly towards the end of the season when figures recorded during the "summer" can seem a long way off and not to be relied on too much. In our experience the best time for one's ratings to be valid is from June to the end of August and certainly doubts creep in when the September mists appear.

The race which we now analyse was run mid-September and the northern trainer, Dandy Nicholls. had adopted his usual scatter-gun approach and was "mob-handed" with no less than four runners, whilst Sir Michael Stoute, always to be feared in handicaps, was relying on a 3yo colt named Main Aim, whose form for this race was quite difficult to assess.

The colt had not run as a 2yo and saw a racecourse for the first time in June, when he won a Class 5 maiden Stakes over 6 furlongs at Salisbury. His next run was in a 7 furlong handicap on a rating of 85, when he maintained his unbeaten record with a narrow win by a neck although he seemed to have a bit in hand. His third outing was on a rating of 90, when he ran in a Class 3 handicap over 7 furlongs at Sandown, where he found no extra at the finish and finished a comfortably beaten third to Brassini. It was thus difficult to gauge his chances in a 6 furlong sprint handicap up against seasoned handicappers. He had 9.4 to carry so did not appear to have been exactly thrown in. However, it was a question of quality against quantity as he outgunned two of the Nicholls' runners who finished second and third.

State Club Handicap - Doncaster

Race 5831

Class 3	6 furs.	Soft		Post race ratings	
	Main Aim	3.9.4	90		95
1 ½	Gift Horse	8.8.13	83		86
3 ½	Joseph Henry	6.9.3	87		86
Hd	Grazeon Gld Blend	5.8.10	80		79
Nk	Atlantic Story	6.9.6	90		88
½	El Dececy	4.9.3	87		84

Pre-race ratings:	Atlantic Story	-4
	Joseph Henry	-3
	Gift Horse	-2
	Stevie Gee	-2
	Swift Princess	-1

Whilst the top rated horse Atlantic Story, is a good and consistent sprinter, we had to entertain doubts about the rating on which we based our assessment as it was achieved back in May on good to firm going. We did not know the reason why it had not run since, but the lack of a recent run is usually a worry. In the event, he ran a good race and, in a big field where the bookmakers paid on the fourth, Atlantic Story managed to finish fifth, beaten a neck for the each-way bet. Joseph Henry and Gift Horse both ran up to their figures but the winner was just too good at the weights.

Extended distance in soft going are difficult to assess, but Joseph Henry's last run had been assessed by us as 85 and as he was on an official rating of 87, we took a figure of 86 as being a sensible compromise and used him as a benchmark. The resultant calculations put Main Aim on a new figure of 95, which didn't seem excessive for what appears to be an improving colt.

Whilst there seemed an adequate reason for Atlantic Story's failure to run to an assessment of -4, which is a very good margin, it is always worth going back to the race where the figure had been established to see if the rating had been justified.

Sporting Index Stakes (Handicap) - York

Race 2172

Class 2		6 furs.	Good to firm		Post race ratings
	Tombi	4.8.13	92		104
2 ½	Atlantic Story	6.8.9	88		94
2 ¼	Hinton Admiral	4.9.2	95		95
½	Machinist	8.9.7	100		98
1	Dream Theme	5.9.2	95		91
1 ½	Malcheek	6.8.10	89		82

In early May it was a bit early for reliable ratings and Atlantic Story's form prior to this race had been on the all-weather. The Raceform post-race comments drew attention to the fact that Hinton Admiral had been dropped in the weights by the Handicapper and he probably wasn't an ideal candidate for the benchmark, but he had kept on well to deprive Machinist of third place and Dandy Nicholls' 8yo has been going long enough for the official to have his mark by now so, for better or for worse, the assessments were made round those two. To put Atlantic Story's rating up by 6 lbs for the 2½ lengths by which he had finished in front of the third horse did not seem excessive although it has to be pointed out that the OH took a lesser view and put Tombi up by 10lbs as against our 12lbs and Atlantic Story went up by only 2 lbs as against our

6 lbs, which meant of course that, in the Doncaster race, Atlantic Story appeared to be rather more well-in than was probably the case.

For those interested in the maths, Hinton Admiral was officially lowered by 1 lb to a new rating of 94. This means that he was allowed 3 lbs (1lbs down for him and 2lbs up for Atlantic Story) for the 2 ¼ lengths between them, whilst Tombi was raised 8lbs (10lbs less Atlantic Story's 2lbs) for the 2½ lengths by which he won. Easy winners are always punished

To have the second, third and fourth in the top six of the assessments in a race like the Portland Handicap at Doncaster but not to include the winner is a bit frustrating, to say the least, especially when the equal-top rated looked all over a winner less that fifty yards out only to get caught in the shadow of the post. Such were the events in mid-September but these things happen.

Ladbroke's Portland Cup - Doncaster

Race 5890

Class 3		5f 140yds	Soft	Post race ratings	
	Hogmaneigh	5.9.6	100	104	
Sh hd	River Falcon	8.8.12	92	94	
Nk	Siren's Gift	4.8.13	93	95	
2	Oldjoesaid	4.9.10	104	103	
Nk	Cheveton	4.8.13	93	91	
Nk	Fathom Five	4.9.6	100	97	

Pre-race assessments:	Siren's Gift	-2
	Hamish McGonagall	-2
	River Falcon	-1
	Oldjoesaid	-1
	Fullanby	-1
	Evens And Odds	-1

The winner Hogmaneigh, was +2 with us and we could not have rated him any higher that that. His four races prior to the Portland Handicap were as follows.

Race 1442   5th of 9 behind Oldjoesaid over 5f 34 yds at Newbury

(This race was featured in Chapter Thirteen, where the extended distances on good to soft going made an accurate assessment difficult and his rating of 97? reflected that)

Race 1809   6th of 25 behind Off the Record over 6 furs at Newmarket where he was given a rating of 95.

Race 2828   4th of 19 behind Holbeck Ghyll for a rating of 98.

This race is in Chapter Eight

Race 5109   8th of 20 behind Tajneed.   No assessment made.

This race featured in Chapter One

Our form line for Hogmaneigh prior to the Portland was therefore:
Hogmaneigh   97? / 95 / 98 / ?

None of this suggested that Hogmaneigh had an outstanding chance of winning the Portland Handicap on an official rating of 100, hence his assessment with us of +2.

For the sake of completion we can tabulate the details of race 1809.

StanJamesuk.Com Stakes (heritage Handicap) - Newmarket

Race 1809

		6 furs.	Good		Post race ratings
Class 2					
	Off The Record	4.8.12	95		98
Hd	Damika	5.9.0	97		99
½	Fullanby	6.9.4	101		101
½	Baby Strange	4.8.4	87		85
½	King's Apostle	4.9.1	98		94
½	Hogmaneigh	5.9.4	101		95

The OH's new ratings were as follows:

Off The Record	99	+4 on previous figure
Damika	100	+3
Fullanby	103	+2
Baby Strange	88	+1
King's Apostle	98	Unchanged
Hogmaneigh	100	-1

It will be seen that our new assessments for Baby Strange, King's Apostle and Hogmaneigh were lowered by 2lbs, 4lbs and 6lbs respectively as compensating for the beaten distances. The OH, on the other hand, makes minimal changes by observing the normal practice that established ratings are seldom lowered by more than a pound or two as has been explained before. To the best of our ability, our ratings are an endeavour to match the form shown by the extended distances, so that our re-assessment for Hogmaneigh of 95 is hopefully a more or less accurate rating for this particular performance. In other words, we are saying that Hogmaneigh, in our opinion, had run some 6lbs below his official rating

This of course, is not written in stone and should the horse put up a higher figure than this in a subsequent race – as he did with a 98 in Race 2828 – then that is the new figure upon which he will be judged. A low assessment means just one thing – that the horse in question has put in a below par performance and is not to be taken as being representative of what he or she can do.

Thus, if a horse sets up consecutive figures of 95 / 97 / 90 / 96 the rating upon which he would be assessed would be 97 because that shows what the horse can do on its best form. If a horse has run four of five times and has run to no higher a figure than say, 98, as was the case with Hogmaneigh, and is now set to "do a 100" we cannot in all conscience give him a higher assessment than +2, which means that he is being set to run 2lbs better than he has done all the year. The fact that he did so is the reason why we are not all as rich as Croesus. Horses improve or everything goes just right during the race and they run right up to their best.

At the risk of labouring the point Hogmaneigh, in Race 5109, and on an official rating of 101, was beaten about six lengths by the winner. His official rating was then reduced by 1lb. The fact that Hogmaneigh had now won on a rating of 100 shows that the handicapper was right not to drop him by any appreciable margin. His main aim is to give a horse a rating which represents the best form of which he thinks the animal is capable and does not in any way attempt to match the ups and downs of actual performances.

For an example of this method of working, one can consult the Racing Post Ratings (RPR) which are published in the Racing Results section of the official Form Book or in the Raceform Update. If one looks at the full result of any particular race it will be found that an RPR figure is given for every horse in the race and this is an assessment calculated to show the exact worth of each performance. It follows that the actual performance of each horse can show quite astonishing variations, which are totally different from the official ratings or even from the way in which we work.

It is of interest to make a direct comparison between the three entirely different approaches and we take as an example the 2008 form record of a useful sprinter Bel Cantor, who, for a slightly different purpose, was highlighted in Chapter Ten.

The top line shows the rating as assessed by RPR, whilst the second line shows the official rating. The third line is that of Weighting for Winners (WW)

RPR   75/82/73/71/85+/79/60/83/81/85+/42/83/86/90/95

OR   67/67/72/72/81/80/80/79/79/79/79/79/77/80/84

WW   --/--/--/--/81/Cl4 3/Cl4 0/77/Cl4 5/Cl4 3/Cl4 0/76/81/84/91

If one wishes to make an exact comparison it has to be borne in mind that the first OR figure of 67 is the rating on which Bel Cantor ran that day. The subsequent OR figures show reaction ratings after the previous outings and may not necessarily have been in time for the next race. The first four races attracted no figure from SH as Bel Cantor was not running in selected races

However, if one takes each individual line of form as a whole, one gets the picture of improvement on Bel Cantor's part. Thus, from an initial RPR rating of 75 Bel Cantor finishes up with a final rating of 95.

In the official ratings he has gone from an early figure of 67 to a final figure of 84, whilst the SH ratings, once its first figure was established, have gone up from 81 to his last figure of 91.

It will be seen that, once a level in the low eighties was reached, Bel Cantor's official rating remained at more or less the same level. This clearly shows the difference between the official figures of those of RPR, where the consecutive ratings show a roller-coaster effect, with each outing getting a figure which seeks accurately to represent its performance on that one day. One gets a clear picture of the ups and downs of Bel Cantor's 2008 career, with a "low" of 42 and a "high" of 95.

Each line of form figures has its own story to tell, but the OR assessments clearly show that the individual ratings do not accurately indicate the "lows" of Bel Cantor's form. The WW form line presents perhaps a more stable view of the gradual improvement through the season but of course, running in non-rated races or when out of the first six are not shown.

This analysis is not intended in any way to highlight the merits or demerits of each form line as each of the three systems has different built-in criteria.   One needs to appreciate this so that differences between the three methods can be clearly understood.

NOTES

Those who decide to compile their own handicap ratings will almost certainly find that the hardest of all races upon which to make a judgment are those where there are over-extended distance between the first six horses, especially when the going is on the easy side. When horses have no chance of winning, one would not expect, or want, them to be forcefully ridden and most of the horses behind the winner tend to just run on at one pace without being unduly pushed. In such circumstances a winning distance of say, 2 ½ lengths, may not be the true guide to the relative merits between the front two, let alone those further behind.

We will have a look at the following race:

Scarborough Handicap - Thirsk

Race 2211

Class 2	5 furs.	Good	Post race ratings		RPR
	Manzila	5.9.3	95	103	110+
2 ½	Ishetoo	4.9.0	92	96	98
2 ¼	Masta Plasta	5.9.4	96	96	94
1 ½	Orpenindeed	5.9.0	92	90	85
3 ¾	Canadian Danehill	6.9.3	95	90?	74
¾	Invincible	4.9.0	92	86?	68

This race was early in the season and our pre-race assessments were non-existent apart from Orpenindeed who was -1

From a point of view of re-assessing the ratings, the first thing to notice is the 11 lengths which covered the first six and one is faced with the difficulty of knowing how much to allow per length. Even a moderate allowance spread over such extended distances would create very doubtful figures. There is also the problem of knowing which horse to use as any kind of benchmark, as apart from Orpenindeed, we had no reliable guide to the level of form. It was almost a guess to use Mastsa Plasta, but he had been very consistent the previous year, was well fancied by the stable and had possibly run up to his official rating.

Which gave us a starting point of leaving him on his OR of 96 but what then?

It did not seem excessive to penalise Ishetoo for the 2¼ lengths between them, which put Ishetoo on 96. Another 4lbs for the winning distance put Manzilla on 103. We could allow Orpenindeed 2lbs for the distance behind the third horse and then we had to consider what to allow for the 3¼ lengths between fourth and fifth. In the event, we dropped Canadian Danehill 5lbs from his official rating and Invincible Force 6lbs, but gave both a question mark because of the doubts. To be honest, we were sceptical of the whole race and waited for the official Ratings List to see what the OH had done.

	Old Rating	**New Rating**	**+ or -**
Manzilla	95	104	+9
Ishetoo	92	93	+1
Masta Plasta	96	96	No change
Orpenindeed	92	92	No change
Canadian Danehill	95	95	No change
Invincible Force	92	90	-2

As can be seen, the winner was duly punished but the rest hardly affected at all. It seems odd that Canadian Danehill received no concession for the 7½ lengths behind Masta Plasta but sometimes that is how it goes. Nevertheless, it was hardly surprising when, 21 days later, Canadian Danehill was still 5 lengths behind Masta Plasta on only 4 lbs better terms, Masta Plasta having won during the interim. It is interesting to note that, on the same day, in the race before Manzila's win, Valery Borzov was penalised 10 lbs for a 3¾ lengths win

N.B. In the race result, the RPR re-assessments are shown to illustrate the way their figures reflect the extended distances.

It is certainly true that weight can bring horses together and mention of Valery Borzov's win above illustrates this. In the race mentioned above, Valery Borzov was penalised 10 lbs and went up from a rating of 82 to one of 92. Sixth in this race was Swinbrook on a rating of 75, who finished 7½ lengths behind the winner. Seventeen days later the pair clashed at Ripon and the result is seen below:

Nick Wilmot-Smith Memorial Handicap - Ripon

Race 2698

Class 3	6 furs.	Heavy		Post race ratings
	Rising Shadow	7.9.12	93	95
¾	Valery Borzov	4.9.11	92	92
¾	Bel Cantor	5.8.12	79	77
1	Swinbrook	7.8.9	76 oh1	73
3	Grazeon Gold Blend	5.8.12	79	74
2	High Curragh	5.9.5	86	80

Swinbrook was 9 lbs better off for the 7½ length beating and this time was beaten only

1¾ lengths thus confirming the form to a nicety.

There will be many times during the season when, whatever system of notation we use, we will find it necessary to use a symbol in our form lines in the database which will be intended to show that a particular horse has failed to finish in the first six in one of our "rated" handicaps, or has been given a tentative rating followed by a question mark, signifying that the assessment is very doubtful. Thus, the form line for one of our listed horses may read 87/90/?/ 88/80?/ 87.

This would indicate ratings of 87 and 90, followed by a run out of the first six in a Class 2 or 3 handicap, a rating of 88, then a "doubtful" rating of 80, followed by a rating of 87. We can often use the "negative" items in this line of form to gain positive information about the horse by using the Raceform comments about the horse in their after-race summary. These comments are often particularly useful in cases where a horse has failed to finish in the first six, as they often contain a strong hint as to why the animal in question failed to do better and this can be useful knowledge in that it might suggest that the horse did not stay the trip, failed to act on the gong, met with interference in running, started slowly, or simply failed to show. In our quest for information all is grist to our mill and any definite indication as to the horse's failure to finish in the first six is often worth a note to the right of the form line on our data sheet. This can be as brief as you like but a note saying "prefers soft" or "not AW" tells you something about the horse's likes and dislikes. If it is found necessary to put a question mark after a tentative rating, there will always be a reason for this and it is usually because the horse has not finished near enough to be given a firm rating. Again, this might be due to the going, or incidents in running and a glance at the Raceform comment will nearly always provide the answer.

The point being made here is that one can never know too much about the performance of any horse in any race and the Raceform experts are there to provide us with the sort of clues we need.

In passing, it can be said that the state of the going is one of the strongest elements affecting the performance of most horses. There are a few admirable creatures which seem able to adapt to any surface but the vast majority are particularly vulnerable to what is under their feet and heavy going can create more upsets than any other factor.

For any "lay" handicapper, the allotting of ratings after a race run in heavy going is very largely a case of sheer guesswork. It is almost impossible to quantify the allowance to be made for a distance of say, 6 lengths, and it is for this reason that a maximum of 7lbs with a query is used in our records. It is a sad sight to see a field of sprinters finish strung out like the runners in a four mile steeplechase and anything further than a very tentative assessment is a waste of time. It is certainly our experience that 5 and 6 furlong handicappers, particularly the better ones, perform to an almost unbelievable standard of consistency but of course, in races where finishes are decided by very narrow margins, the top rated horses cannot always do as we expect and it is perfectly possible for a horse to be top rated, yet finish fifth having run to the top of the form. It is therefore a great pity when these sturdy and reliable campaigners run well below form on going more fitted to an Irish chase.

In Chapter Three we discussed Race 5310, where the winner was Perfect Fight, a filly who can really be said to like to get her toe in. She is a much better horse on soft going as has been demonstrated by two wins at Goodwood on soft ground. In Race 5310 she won by 3 lengths and we had some difficulty in judging the worth of the win. According to Raceform she drew clear in the last furlong and we allowed 2lbs per length for a total increase of 6lbs above her official rating to put her on our level of 83. When she next ran, in the Derrick Smith's Oury Clark Free Bus Pass Stakes (Handicap) – a rather wonderful name for any contest – she was on an official rating of 84 which made her +1 with us.

Race 5930

	Class 2	6 furs.	Soft	Post race ratings	
	Perfect Flight	3.8.10	84	91
2 ½	Masai Moon	4.9.6	92	94
2 ½	King's Caprice	7.8.13	85	82
½	Little Pete	3.9.3	91	87
½	Baldemar	3.9.0	88	84
¾	Sir Edwin Landseer	8.9.4	90	85

The pre-race ratings were:

King's Caprice	-3
Little Pete	-2
Osiris Way	--
Perfect Flight	+1

On the face of it King's Caprice, who had come down in the weights, looked a cast iron each way bet and was backed down from 8-1 to 6-1. He ran quite well to finish third but neither he nor Masai Moon was a match for Perfect Flight who loved the going and had won previously over the course. The filly has probably come on since her earlier win but it is hard to escape the niggling thought that we under-rated that performance and that the rating of 83 was too low. One consolation is that the OH didn't do much better and rated her at 84. However, this rather exemplifies the fact that, in soft going, it is very easy to misjudge the worth of a win and one must be prepared for results which don't go by the book. Unfortunately, one cannot say one will know better next time because it is not wise to do more than make an educated estimate and treat the result as it stands. Being wise after the event is not a luxury extended by bookmakers and, strictly on the figures, Perfect Flight had a bit to do. Her connections would have been delighted with the starting price of 11-2. Improving fillies in the Autumn.................

CHAPTER SEVENTEEN

The form line of each horse shown in our database is a microcosm, representing each animal's performances during the season. Inevitably there will be highs and lows as it cannot be expected that the horse will run to its top level every time. Such variations are caused by a variety of differing circumstances such as distance, going, incidents in running and of course, the horse's well being. Nevertheless, the line of numbers and symbols can be very revealing to the experienced observer but of course, the main intention is to indicate the best that the horse can do.

A guiding principle of form study is to back a horse to do what it has done before and, if a sprinter has a highest figure of 98 over a reasonable number of appearances, it is always to be hoped that, barring accidents and given the right conditions, it will run to that figure again. The basis for compiling a short list of "candidates" is to highlight those few horses that are set by the OH to do less than has been achieved before. Any horse which has set up consistently high ratings represents a good betting opportunity if and when its official rating is less than its best recorded figure. This can happen when a horse, after setting up a couple of good figures, then proceeds to run slightly below that level and this might be due to running out of its class, on unsuitable going or experiencing a couple of unlucky runs when badly drawn. As a consequence, the OH will perhaps lower its rating by two or three pounds over a period of time and there comes a time when it is being set to run to a rating which is some pounds below its best recorded level.

Therein lies the rub. As has been mentioned before, the one question which bedevils the assessments is how far does one go back to make a comparison between what the horse has done before and what it is being asked to do today? A high rating set up in say April, is a very doubtful quality to take into a race in August, especially if there have been three or four outings during the interim when the horse in question has failed to run to its previous high figure. One is faced with the possibility that the horse may have deteriorated during that time and is no longer capable of running to its best form.

If one is faced with this dilemma it is usually a good idea to see what its current official rating is, as the handicapper will have certainly taken into account the intervening races.

If say, a horse has set up what appeared to be a reliable figure of 88 and had then run a series of races without reaching that level, it might be that its current official rating is now 78, which is a sure sign that the horse has, in fact, deteriorated and cannot be expected to run at its former level. One has to ignore the previous figure.

However, it can sometimes happen that the intervening races have not shown the OH any concrete evidence that the horse has "gone" and the animal in question is on very much the same rating level as it was two months ago. If the horse's latest performance shows any degree of promise that it is still in form, it would be no surprise to see it produce a performance right up to its previous mark. Because a horse has had several un-rated (with us) outings since setting up a good figure, it does not necessarily follow that it is no longer capable of running to its top figure and very often the best bets have come about due to this circumstance.

The best form line to see is one which shows a gradual rise in the assessments, and if this coincides with an upgrade in the official ratings, you have an infallible sign that the horse is improving and very often, the OH finds it difficult to keep pace with such improvement.

A simple case of getting expert guidance from the OH is that of a moderate sprinter named Cape Royal who had early figures of 85/83/79 with us, followed by a string of eleven outings in Class 4 and 5 races, during which we had no accurate record of his progress or otherwise. It was a matter of seeing what its latest official rating was and, finding it to be 77, it is clear that, should he return to Class 2 or 3 races, we could not expect him to run within 7lbs of his earlier ratings. Thus, without any arduous wading through the form book, one has an expert's view of what can be expected and much time is saved.

Conversely, a quite useful sprinter Crystany, started the season in a decent Class 2 handicap and earned a rating of 92. After this, the connection aimed rather higher and Crystany took on Listed Company in three races over 5 and 6 furlongs. She then ran on the all-weather by which time we had obviously lost touch with her. Once more, a check on her official rating was sufficient to put us in the picture. At the last count, she was on an official rating of 95, which tells us that if Crystany reverts to handicap class, we could confidently expect her to at least run up to our early rating of 92.

When one is uncertain of the current status of a horse which has good early figures but has since run in races beyond our terms of reference, a check with the official ratings will often suffice to make things clear. A very useful gelding Damika, was shown in our form line to have assessments of 96/97/99/99 and looked a good sprinting prospect. He then ran in a non-handicap event, a race over 7 furlongs and two Listed races, which were shown in our form line, but gave no indication as to his current status were he to run in a Class 2 or 3 handicap. We had no clue from his last four races but his OR now stood at 105, which clearly demonstrates that Damika was reliably considered to have improved on his rating and was now one of the best sprinters in the country. It bears mentioning that his official rating in April was 95, so his current rating confirms considerable improvement during the season. One of Damika's early races is dealt with in Chapter Three (Race 1300).

Fortunately, when preparing the pre-race assessments for any race, the official rating you are using to compare against your own figures will occasionally be markedly different from what you expect and the resultant big plus or minus will be sufficient warning that your 1st rating may be suspect.

For more on this subject please see Chapter Two.

NOTES

CHAPTER EIGHTEEN

The Ayr Gold Cup, run in September, is one of the most prestigious handicaps sprints to take place during the year and, needless to say, is one of the most difficult to solve. The race is often the last chance saloon of the season for top handicap sprinters and there are always plenty of runners. As it is late in the season, the Handicapper has got the measure of practically every horse taking part and the difference between our ratings and those of the OH are usually very tight. As with all races, one compares the figures with the intention of making up a short list from which we hope the winner will come. In the case of the Ayr Gold Cup, this "short" list can often be quite lengthy as there can easily be a dozen or so horses within a pound of each other.

Any horse can run a really good race and yet fail to reach the first six, so close is the contest. The day before the Gold Cup there is a consolation race known as the Silver Cup which acts as a consolation event for those who could not get into the big race itself. It goes without saying that this race is as tricky as the Gold Cup, but at least it does have the virtue of acting as a good guide to the main event as far as the effect of the draw is concerned and can often show which side of the course is favoured.

Ayr Silver Cup - Ayr

Race 6069

Class 2		6 furs.	Heavy		Post race ratings
	Against The Grain	5.9.0	82		90
2 ¾	Harrison George	3.9.4	88		90
Nk	Joseph Henry	6.9.6	88		89
Hd	Bel Cantor	5.9.7	89		89
3	Marvellous Value	3.9.8	92		87?
Nk	Protector	7.9.8	90		85?

Our pre-race ratings

were as follows:

Gift Horse	-3
Burning Incense	-2
Bel Cantor	-2
Thebes	-1
Stevie Gee	-1

With heavy going and late in the season, this was pretty much a non-event as far as our ratings were concerned. In a hotly contested race like the Ayr Gold Cup one certainly wouldn't expect to find 6 lengths separating the first five horses to finish. As can be seen, the only one of our top six horses to reach a place was the ever consistent Bel Cantor, who has shown steady improvement all the year. The winner has been showing decent form over 7 furlongs but had no form over 6 furlongs this year. Harrison George ran a good race when sixth to Pearly Way in the Goodwood Stewards' Cup (Race 4586) but the best we could give him there was a mark of 85, so he was +3 for this race.

Joseph Henry is an old hand at these handicap sprints, as would befit an inmate of the Nicholls' stable, but his season's figures of 92/90/?/89/85/86 did not indicate that he was improving, although his early assessment of 92 certainly gave him a great chance here and he probably ran right up to our rating of 89

Four of the first six home were drawn very low and the race was probably decided as much by the draw as the state of the going. This result would doubtless cause the Official Handicapper to give a rueful shrug of his shoulders and we have to do the same.

Our pre-race ratings for the main event, the Ayr Gold Cup, were too close to call but we give them for the sake of rounding the circle.

Pre-race ratings:

	Baby Strange	-2
	River Falcon	-2
	Evens and Odds	-1
	Tajneed	--
	Knot In Wood	--
	Northern Fling	--
	Tamagin	--
	Turnkey	--
	Ishetoo	--

Ayr Gold Cup - Ayr

Race 6104

Class 2	6 furs.	Heavy		Post race ratings
	Regal Parade	4.9.1	99	105
2 ¼	Tajneed	5.8.12	96	97
Nse	Confuchias	4.9.2	100	101
Nk	Knot In Wood	6.9.4	102	102
¾	Skhilling Spirit	5.8.9	93	92
Hd	Patavellian	10.8.11	95	94

That man Nicholls strikes again, with first and second, but whilst we had Tajweed in our top assessments, the same could not be said of Regal Parade, whose best form, very useful though it was, had all been over 7 furs and a mile. Judging by the result of this race and the Ayr Silver Cup, the heavy going demanded a horse that could stay at least 7 furlongs and quite a few of our top rated horses would find that beyond them.

Knot In Wood is a very game and consistent performer and leaving him on the OH mark of 102 fitted in well with our own previous ratings for this horse. (He suffered no ill effects from a good run in the Gold Cup as he won a stakes race the next day.). The rest, bearing in mind the conditions, were subject to minimal adjustments although the winner goes up to 105, a plus of 6lbs on his official rating. The 2¼ lengths win had to be worth at least that.

Regal Parade has had a varied career after being bought as a yearling for 430,000 gns and sent to Mark Johnston's yard, where he started off well enough last year to win three fairly minor races and ran over distances from 7 furlongs to 1¼ miles but, after his wins he went completely off the boil and finished up with the dreaded Timeform "squiggle" and the comment, "not one to trust".

He was sold out of Johnston's yard for 16,000 gns and went to Dandy Nicholls' yard. Nicholls has a reputation for bringing out the best in other stable's cast-offs, so it wasn't exactly jaw dropping when he produced Regal Parade to win the Buckingham Palace Stakes over 7 furlongs at the Royal Ascot meeting. On his last outing before the Ayr Gold Cup however, Regal Parade finished 10th in the Totesport Mile at Goodwood and there could not have been many people, apart perhaps the indefatigable Nicholls, who would have imagined that he was to come on from that and win the Ayr Gold Cup in September against specialist sprinters.

Unfortunately, the form student has little or no chance of making sense out of all this and few outside the stable could have fancied Regal Parade at Ayr, although at 18-1 he was probably not entirely unbacked. It could easily be said that, if the going has been good to firm, the result would almost certainly have been entirely different but that's racing.

Our next race, at Haydock, presented many horses who had found conditions beyond them at Ayr, a chance to redeem themselves. As in politics, a week is a long time in racing and with little or no rain, the going was far better suited to specialised sprinters than the mud bath at Ayr.

Betfred.com Handicap - Haydock

Race 6289

			Good to firm	Post race ratings	
	Chief Editor	4.9.3		97	103
4 ½	Barney Mc Grew	5.8.12		92	94
1 ½	Lipocco	4.9.6		100	98
Sh Hd	Misaro	7.8.12		92	90
½	Cute Ass	3.8.13		95	92
¾	Burning Incense	5.8.6		86	82

Class 2   6 furs.

Pre-race ratings:	Burning Incence	-3	Sixth
	Chief Editor	-1	Won
	Barney Mc Grew	--	Second
	Everymanforhimself	--	
	Bel Cantor	--	
	Joseph Henry	--	
	Musaalem	--	
	Mac Gille Eoin	--	

The pre-race ratings, with only 3lbs separating the top eight "candidates" hardly deserved a medal, despite including the first, second and sixth, but there is an instructive lesson to be learned from the winner, Chief Editor. Early in the season, he had earned a rating of 98, which put him on the -1 mark. Since then however, he had not attracted our attention as far as getting a later rating was concerned, and it was a question as to whether he was capable of reproducing that earlier figure. He had run in three race since then, which were:

Second on a rating of 98 in the John Smith Conditions Stakes over 5 furlongs on soft going.

Last of 6 in the Group 3 Flying Five Stakes at the Curragh when he was quite obviously out of his depth.

13/21 in the Portland Handicap at Doncaster on a rating of 97, and this is the all-important guide to his well being. The Raceform race reader's notes are very informative.

"Shaped better than his final position........Held off the pace, he had conditions to suit (soft going) but got no luck when his rider was looking for a way through inside the final two furlongs and the cause was soon given up".

This was a good indication that the gelding had not lost his form and so had a good chance at the weights in this Haydock race but of course, no better than quite a few others. The Official Handicapper could hardly have been overjoyed with the winning distances of 4½ and 1½ lengths respectively, making a total of six lengths between the first and third, hardly the sort of margins to be expected in a Class 2 sprint run on good/firm going.

Chief Editor has seemed to give very indication that he was best on a soft surface but showed here that he acts just as well on good ground. Nevertheless, the result goes to show that a recent race is often an excellent guide as to whether a horse is likely to confirm earlier form.

The legendary Lester Piggott was remembered in our next race.

Betfred Lester Piggott "Start to Finish" Handicap - Haydock

Race 6290

Class 2	5 furs.	Good - firm	Post race ratings	
	Judd Street	6.9.4	96	103
2	Fantasy Explorer	5.8.7	85	87
¾	Quiet Elegance	3.8.10	89	89
Hd	Secret Asset	3.8.13	92	91
Sh Hd	Tom's Laughter	4.9.5	97	96
½	Royalist	3.8.6	85	83

Pre-race ratings:	Fol Hollow	-4
	Prior Warning	-4
	Fantasy Explorer	-2
	Fyodor	--

We all learn from experience, which teaches that one swallow does not make a summer and that a pretty abysmal showing of the rated horses does not condemn figures built up over a season to the waste bin. Even so, it was a very disappointing race from our point of view and as three of the first six to finish had not finished in the first six of a Class 2 or 3 sprint handicap and thus had no rating, one is left with the impression that the majority of the runners had, for some inexplicable reason, ran below form. However, there are inevitably many ifs and buts surrounding races run late in the season and this was no exception. One fairly important point can perhaps be made by reminding readers that horses do not make the top or near top of the handicap without decent form to their credit and Judd Street had done enough to justify his 9.4 mark, higher than any other runner bar Tom's Laughter. In his last three races, Judd Street had run in a Listed race and finished a decent fifth in a handicap on the all-weather at Great Leighs before finishing a very creditable 5/14 in the Group 3 World Trophy at Newbury behind such redoubtable performers as Moorhouse Lad, Wi Dud, Tom's Laughter and Look Busy, all at level weights except the 3yo Look Busy with a 1 lb WFA allowance. The Raceform race reader was sufficiently impressed to say, " battled on well……….he is likely to bid for a repeat win in the Listed Rous Stakes at Newmarket next" This was good sprinting form by anyone's standards, so it was not too surprising that he won this Class 2 handicap, reversing placings with Tom's Laughter on 1lb better terms.

We conclude our review of the 2008 sprint handicaps with the following.

National Express York Sprint Cup (Heritage Handicap) - Musselburgh

Race 6653

Class 2		5 furs.	Post race ratings	
	Hamish McGonagall	3.9.1	95	99
Nk	Cheveton	4.8.13	93	96
Hd	Captain Dunne	3.9.1	95	97
½	Hogmaneigh	5.9.10	104	104
¾	River Falcon	8.9.1	95	94
½	Tombi	4.9.10	104	103

Pre-race ratings:	Hamish McGonagall	-2
	Captain Dunne	-1
	Hogmaneigh	--
	Ishetoo	--
	Tombi	--

With four of our top five in the front six, including the 11-1 winner, this was as good as one can expect, especially at the tail-end of the season.

It was good too see such a well exposed horse winning a prestige handicap and there was further encouragement for support by the Raceform comments for his last two races.

Race 4240   Ayr Jul 21   "Hamish McGonagall looked in good shape…………He proved a disappointment………….(but) has been a progressive sort and is worth another chance"

Race 5890   Doncaster Sept 13   "Hamish McGonagall, one of only four 3yo's in the line-up, showed up well to a furlong out………he will be happier back over a sharp 5f"

Top rated and a course and distance winner, Hamish McGonagall was a sound each way prospect and came through in the final furlong to win a nice race. Cheveton had won five races on the trot but had not qualified for a rating with us until Race 5890 (Chapter Fifteen) when he had finished fifth behind Hogmaneigh who was conceding 7lbs. On that form we were not able to give Cheveton a higher rating than 91, so here he was on an assessment of +2 and not in our top five. He was 4lbs better off with Hogmaneigh and reversed the placings with that horse, top earn a post race rating of 95. Ishetoo, actually finished 7th so the ratings can be said to have worked out very well, a pleasant way to wind up the season.

[The following is a partial reprint from my book *Sprint Handicaps Explained* but the same sentiments apply and are perhaps, worth repeating].

We would like to remind readers that all the assessments made in this book and any opinions expressed were made after the races were run and no amendments have been made in the light of subsequent happenings. In other words this book is a pure "hands-on" effort and reproduces exactly what the reader will have to do during the season should they attempt a similar exercise. As a natural consequence of working in this way, we proved to be wrong in many cases but the book is intended to be an honest attempt to show the sort of difficulties which beset the private handicapper and should be considered in that light.

Readers will note that a constant problem arises in making a decision as to how far to go back in deciding upon a horse's level of performance. There is no easy answer to this as one is attempting to forecast whether or not any particular horse will reproduce his or her best figure that may have been set up some time before. We have tried to deal with this in this book and suggested various ways of dealing with this vexed question and came to the same conclusion as countless form students have come to over the years i.e. that recent form is probably best. If however, a horse has returned good figures and there is no clear evidence of deteriorating, it is wise to include it in one's pre-race assessments. If it has shown up well in recent races, even if out of the first six, it would be foolish to discount its chance.

We come now to the question of which time of the year to follow the ratings. A lot depends on the going and current British Summers are not of the greatest help in that direction. If the going remains consistently good, or good to firm, one can have every confidence that the assessments will prove a valuable guide. We would suggest however, that races after mid-September should be treated with care, as horses who have done little during the summer months, can reproduce form shown in the spring.

Many good winners were indicated during the year by our assessments but it has to be borne in mind that not everyone would have got the same results and they could have bettered them or fared worse. Not every form student will interpret a result in the same way and mis-judgments abound. Students should avoid the practice of up-grading the rating of any horse because it has run well against a horse who is on its way up through the ratings. It may or may not do the same but amending one's assessments in the light of future happenings can prove disastrous. You are urged to work in a logical and methodical manner in your interpretation of every result and always bear in mind that assessments made in the light of previous figures and supported by other horses involved in the finish can usually be relied upon.

Close attention should be paid to the official Ratings List which is published in the Raceform Update or in the general Form Book once a week. These will often indicate a horse which is due for a rise in their OR but which will not take effect until the following Saturday. Such animals will be running at their old level and if you have it upgraded in its previous race, you have the makings of a good bet. At least you will able to say with confidence that such and such a horse is well in at the weights without using guesswork.

As was explained early in this book we have analysed only Class 2 and Class 3 handicaps which seemed useful for the purposes of demonstrating certain facets of handicapping. We did not include any Class 4, 5 or 6 handicaps as it was felt that there was little to be gained from their inclusion. We have found however, that there was an overlap in that many horses who ran in Class 2 or 3 handicaps often descended to Class 4 and there was thus a body of collateral form which was not taken into account. It is suggested therefore, that if time permits, Class 4 races should be included in one's analyses, not just for the sake of completeness, but in order to keep tabs on those who stray into hitherto unknown waters.

Making the selection

The Timeform organisation, whose race ratings are highly respected and used extensively by racing's professionals, has often stated that their top two rated horses include the winner in approximately 50% of the races covered. One has to accept that many of these successes would be short priced, stand-out winners of what might be termed "easy" races. Timeform do not say what sort of average they get in sprint handicaps where the living is not easy.

We amateurs can hardly hope to compete on level terms with such a professional and dedicated set-up with their talented staff of expert race readers and their use of statistical data. However, we can be well satisfied if our figures include the winner and perhaps a placed horse in our top four in a satisfactory number of races.

In making a final selection based on our own form assessments one has to weigh up all the various factors, especially the going which is probably the biggest element to affect a horse's running. Never be put off by the price. Horses with good form are often a bigger price than they ought to be simply because punters tend to forget earlier form. Your records will show you all you need to know about any particular horse and you will be in possession of real "information", not the kind you pick up from the milkman.

Few horses win with a big "plus" figure and if your figures show that a horse is set to carry 5 or 6 lbs more than your figures show it has done for its last three outings – then forget it. Exceptions to this can be a horse who is carrying a substantial penalty but which is at the top of its form.

Oddly enough, one also has to be wary of a horse with a big minus figure, indicating that it is carrying a lot less weight than its BEST form figure. This may have been set up in the distant past and if the animal in question has run well below par in recent races, let this be enough to steer you away. The minus figure is simply because the Official Handicapper has seen fit to give the horse a considerable drop in its OR and this is never a good sign. It is possible that the horse may suddenly show a return to form because it now has all the conditions in its favour and we have to watch things very carefully to see if there is a good reason why the horse might now show its best form and a few minutes spent in investigation is always worthwhile.

The ideal situation for us is where we have a good, reliable rating for every horse taking part, but some people might be content with taking only the first five or six in the betting forecast into consideration and this is a matter for each person. Nevertheless, and where they are available, it is preferable to have a rating for every horse as one would not wish to miss a big priced winner out of inertia.

We will take notice of such pointers as course winners, the class of the race, the draw and perhaps riding arrangements, but the biggest factor will be our form assessments. Horses win when they are well handicapped and we will be in a better position than most to tell when this is so. Have every confidence that the comparatively small amount of homework will have a built-in bonus if only for the reason that you will be a specialist with real expertise in a little understood aspect of a great sport. Good luck.

The Finish